We'll always have
that night in Berlin

Robin

Praise for *Words You Don't Know*

"Veni, vidi, legi," ~ *Julius Caesar*

"The lyf so short, the booke so longe" ~ *Geoffrey Chaucer*

"What blatherskitery is this?" ~ *William Shakespeare*

"The Pobble who has no readers
Had once as many as me;
When they said "Some day you may lose them all;"
He replied "Fish, fiddle-de-dee!"
~ *Edward Lear*

"This is not a book to be tossed aside lightly. It should be thrown away with great force." ~ *Dorothy Parker*

"A slavish concern for the composition of words is the sign of a bankrupt intellect. Be gone, odious wasp! You smell of decayed syllables." ~ *Norton Juster*

Disclaimer: As is the case with most "praise for" pages, none of the above people read this book. Nevertheless, some of the content of this book has been posted on the web site WordsYouDontKnow.com prior to the rigorous editing and reworking it has undergone. Here are some of the comments it elicited:

"Do you know what you would see a hypothecary about? Have you stared down into a joola? Ever come across a jigget of sheep? Has someone called you a slubberdegullion to your face? Learn these and many more words from blogger Robin Bloor's fun 10 Words You Don't Know series of posts. Perhaps the most entertaining is the one where Bloor provides explanatory limericks with his definitions." ~ *Kári Tulinius, a.k.a. Kattullus, on Metafilter.*

"Damn, this was a good article. However, I did know the etymology of *sophisticated*, *robot* and *salary*." ~ *Obnoxio The Clown*

"I love these words…keep them coming!" ~ *Sarah*

WORDS YOU DON'T KNOW

BY ROBIN BLOOR

Humorous Essays Involving Rare Words,
Swear Words, Wrong Words, Long Words,
Curse Words, Terse Words, Legal Words, Regal
Words, Tech Words, Sex Words,
Eponyms and Retronyms

LITTLE CROW

LITTLE CROW

Published by
LITTLE CROW PRESS
Austin, Texas
www.littlecrowpress.com

ISBN 978-0-9789791-1-9

Library of Congress Control Number: 2009935157

PRINTED IN THE UNITED STATES OF AMERICA

www.WordsYouDontKnow.com

DEDICATION

This book is dedicated to all those discerning and elozable individuals who have had the good taste to purchase it. They are the salt of the earth, the bedrock of society, the guardians of culture and an inspiration to their peers. But enough of this honeyfuggling. On with the book!

TABLE OF CONTENTS

—∾—

I

FIMBLEFAMBLES

"Every vice has its excuse ready." ~ Publilius Syrus

We could call this part of the book the exordium or we could call it the prolegomenon. It would be a bit of a let down to call this anything as mundane as the preface, the introduction, the foreword or the prologue, because those words are all too familiar and this book purports to be about "words you don't know." I'm betting that you've never met with *exordium* and *prolegomenon* before. They have roughly the same meaning. They refer to a preliminary essay or set of words that haunt the beginning of a treatise or learned book.

I don't think of this collection of verbose essays as something as grandiose as that, so I cannot regard this as a true exordium (or prolegomenon)—even though this is where the book starts. In reality, it's nothing more than a set of excuses I've cooked up to cover a potential situation wherein some impertinent individual catches you perusing this book and asks, "Why are you reading that?"

Let me tell you a story. One day I wrote a posting for my blog (HaveMacWillBlog.com) with the title "10 Words You Don't Know." I have no idea why I wrote it. That day I decided I wanted to write something whimsical and I stumbled onto a list of rarely used words, so I wrote about some of them. The posting quickly became the most read item that I have ever written—with tens of thousands of readers visiting my web site to read it. I cannot explain why the posting was so popular and why so many people were attracted to it. Similarly, I cannot know why you would want to read this book, but clearly you do, otherwise you wouldn't be reading these words.

Consequently, just in case you have no idea why you're reading it either, I'm providing you with a set of reasons—excuses, really. So this is not an exordium at all. It's a collection of fimblefambles: ten lying excuses for you to use if you need to explain why you're reading this book. I sincerely hope at least one or two are useful.

But let me pause just a moment to explain this "ten" thing. Why is the number *10* so satisfying? Why is 5 excuses too few and 14 too many? You could chalk it up, I guess, to the fact that most of us have 10 fingers. Perhaps David Letterman has conditioned us to expect all of life's little perplexities to arrive in neatly ordered lists of 10. Maybe it was Bo Derek running down the beach in that carneous (flesh-colored) swimsuit—in slow motion no less—that branded the number *10* in our collective psyches. Whatever the reason, the number *10* seems to be hardwired into my brain, and probably yours, as a solid, pleasing quantity. Not too little and not too much—just right.

Now. On with the fimblefambles!

"I found it."

This is a very credible excuse. People are always leaving or abandoning books at airports, on airplanes, and on trains. Consequently, other people are always picking them up, browsing through them, and maybe even reading them. As long as your copy of this book looks reasonably well thumbed, you should get away with this fiction. You can then respond to your inquisitor—the one who dared to ask why you were reading this book—by saying,

"Gosh, haven't you any idea what the word *fronglemenser* means? It's a person who tries to engage you in conversation when you're much more interested in reading a book."

"I know the author. Look. It's signed!"

To prove it, you can show them the front page of the book where I've printed a personal message to you and added a signature. And, I promise you, if anyone calls to ask whether I really signed the book, I'll tell them that I did.

I was inspired to print that message and signature by a friend of mine. Having written his first book, he sent me a copy, along with a sticker—on which a lovely message and his signature had been printed—and directions to stick it in the front of the book. "What a useful idea," I thought to myself.

Books are worth more if they are signed by the author, so maybe people will value this book more if I print my signature in the front along with a personal message.

Even better, I can now avoid going on a book-signing tour, because the books are already signed.

"I'm learning English as a second language and this is recommended reading for the course."

This is a whopper. Nobody in his right mind and teaching English as a second language is going to recommend this book, unless they simply hate foreigners and want them all to go back to the place from whence they came. If you really are learning English as a second language and your teacher gives you this book, change your course.

Nevertheless, this claim is credible. The title of the book *almost* implies that the words it contains are words you should know.

3

Bear in mind that this excuse may require a little skill, as you may have to pretend that English is indeed your second language. If you don't think you can carry that off, try a different fimblefamble.

"Oprah Winfrey recommended it."

She didn't. But it's no secret that Oprah's book recommendations are very powerful endorsements, so I'm slipping this fimblefamble in as a simple act of self-promotion. Just the rumor that Oprah may have been a little partial to this book will do me no harm whatsoever.

I'm hoping you'll use this excuse much more than any of the others. After all, if Oprah had recommended this book, it's probably worth reading. So… Let's all assume she did.

"My spouse bought it for me."

If you're feeling a little uncomfortable that you've been caught reading this book, then this is the fimblefamble for you. Everyone knows that spouses buy each other lousy presents. It's in the wedding vow somewhere.

Come out with this and your inquisitor will naturally feel a certain amount of sympathy. Then they'll start to discuss the lousy present their spouse got them the last time their birthday came round, and—voilà—you've successfully changed the subject.

"I'm trying to improve my vocabulary."

Of course, you're not. But your inquisitor doesn't know that, and improving your vocabulary is often thought of as something worth doing. So it is a lie worth telling. Vocabularies should be big and everyone ought do whatever they can to augment them. Have you noticed how

4

you never run into people who claim that they're trying to decrease their vocabulary?

"I love the English language and I'm hoping to improve my knowledge of it."

I hate to admit this, but if you read this book, you might actually improve your knowledge of English. It's not written with that aim in mind, so don't get your hopes up, but it may have a little impact in that direction. Writing it certainly improved my knowledge of English, but (and I'm not lying here) it improved my knowledge of Greek much more. But you can hardly use "I'm trying to improve my knowledge of Greek" as a credible excuse for reading this book. No one's gonna buy that.

"I wanted to find out more about the origin of words."

In which case you should have bought an etymological dictionary. Actually, this book will provide a little data here and there about the origin of some words, but it isn't organized and it won't develop your knowledge much.

You will discover though, possibly to your complete surprise, that English is a whoring slut of a language, happy to consort with just about any other language it meets. Our beloved English can be forgiven for inheriting words from root languages like Greek, Latin, German and French, but Polish, Serbo-Croat, Hindi, Arabic, Swahili, Urdu, Aborigine, Chinese, and Japanese? Does the lady have no shame?

It's not her fault. The simple fact is that English verbs don't conjugate much. The nouns have no gender and there's no declension. The adjectives normally don't have to agree with the nouns in any way. There are almost no rules of spelling and the rule for creating a plural (add an *s*) works for almost any foreign word. If any of the very few rules of English get in the way, it's okay to break them. Put that all together and there's almost no way to prevent new words getting into the language from elsewhere. All that has to happen is for people to start using them.

"I wonder just how many of these words I know."

Face it; you don't know any of them. And if you do, then "you're a better man than I am, Gunga Din." You won't run into many of these words even if you consume the complete works of William Shakespeare and read the *New York Times* from cover to cover every day for a year.

Not that it matters. This is a fimblefamble after all, and it's a good one if you can carry it off. Pretend you're an English Professor from an obscure university in Australia and read out the word *omoplatoscopy*. "Ah yes, I seem to remember that John Harvey Higgins wrote a dissertation on the influence of omoplatoscopy in early Chinese society."

"I bought it for the bookshelf."

This is the fimblefamble par excellence for this book: "I just wanted to see its spine on my bookshelf next to Dostoyevsky's *Crime and Punishment* and Herman Melville's *Moby Dick*."

Unless they have actually read this book, people are going to think that it's some kind of serious, learned tome, and what better to do with a learned tome than to flip through it so you have some idea what it contains and, then, consign it to the bookshelf forever to gather dust.

I heartily recommend this fimblefamble.

II

THE FIRST TEN WORDS YOU DON'T KNOW

"The larger the island of knowledge, the longer the shoreline of wonder." ~ Ralph W. Sockman

This collection is the one that I created on a whim and the one that attracted so much attention. Its lure probably came from the challenge implied in the appellation, "Words You Don't Know." Some readers of this section will surely know one or two of these words, because that's just the way of the world. But most of you will not know any of them and, to be honest, you will not find them hard to forget. I've forgotten most of them already. Here's the pioneering list of ten obscure and strange words, randomly selected from a much longer list I keep:

Anopisthography

This refers to the practice of writing on just one side of the paper. When I have a notebook that opens left-to-right, I'm not an anopisthographist, but when the pages are bound at the top, I convert to anopisthography immediately. I'll bet most of you are the same. I'll also bet that all of you suffer from Post-It® anopisthography. Only a curmudgeonly pinchpenny would fail to do so.

Quomodocunquize

Quomodocunquize is a word for recessionary times. I'm hoping it will see much greater usage now that so many of us are impecunious. It means *to make money by any possible means*. Naturally, that includes both immoral and amoral means, but could also include ingenious means, such as making money from doing nothing more than writing about unusual words.

Jentacular

What could be more jentacular than the smell of bacon and eggs cooking on the stove and the rustle of cornflakes as you pour them into the bowl? The answer is nothing, really, as long as you live in America or the United Kingdom. However, if you live in Scandinavia, such things are not jentacular at all—although the sight of sliced cheeses and cold meats on a plate certainly are. *Jentacular* means *relating to breakfast.*

Pigmentocracy

From the presidential perspective, 2008 saw the end of pigmentocracy in America, pigmentocracy being government by those of one skin color. To no one's surprise, pigmentocracy tends to be the rule in most countries. The United States is now one of the few exceptions.

Squaliform

Squaliform means *shaped like a shark.* It's the kind of word you don't get to use very often, even if you know it. All sharks are, by definition, squaliform. But not many other denizens of the deep are similarly shaped. Also, should you actually be snorkeling in shark-infested waters and see the clichéd shark fin sticking out of a wave, you're more likely to explete the unanticipated presence of the shark than to announce calmly, "Why, I believe there's something squaliform coming this way."

Quickhatch

A quickhatch is not what it sounds like—not to me at any rate. That is, it's not a chick emerging prematurely from its egg. It's something else entirely. Hugh Jackman portrays a human quickhatch in the X-Men movies, with the latest movie in the series being very specifically about Hugh Jackman's acquisition of his quickhatchness.

A quickhatch is a wolverine. Apparently, the word derives from the American Indian—probably Cree—word, *kwiihkwahaacheew*. Sounds like a sneeze to me.

Think about the movie poster we could have had if this word had stayed in its original language …

Gossypiboma

I love really, really specialized words and *gossypiboma* is a great exemplar. A gossypiboma is a surgical sponge accidentally left inside a patient's body.

It's a surprising fact that patients occasionally leave the operating theater with a little souvenir from the surgical team. Statistics suggest that these oversights occur about 30 times per week in the U.S. and a couple of times a week in the U.K.—the disparity in frequency being attributable to the fact that Americans undergo vastly more operations per person than the British. Things left behind include swabs, clips, screws, and surgical implements. Only the first on this list is actually a gossypiboma—the rest don't warrant a word of their own.

Noxal

When people discover, to their dismay, that they are the proud owner of a gossypiboma, they are likely to regard it as a noxal distinction. As a word, *noxal* has, on occasion, been used to mean *noxious*, but the correct meaning of this adjective is a little more specialized than that: *pertaining to damage or wrongful injury from an object—or possibly an animal—belonging to someone else.*

Hypothecary

I'm sure you're well aware what an apothecary is. *Apothecary* is an alternative word for pharmacist. A hypothecary, however, is not a hyperactive pharmacist. It's much more topical than that. A hypothecary is a mortgagee—someone who loans money to house buyers. Under normal circumstances, hypothecaries simply make a living by gathering interest payments on the mortgage.

In recent times, hypothecaries bundled up tranches (i.e., slices) of property loans into derivatives and sold them to banks all over the world. This created an unsustainable financial bubble. The bursting of the bubble gave rise to a stock market crash and a huge increase in unemployment. This left many people with little option but to quomodocunquize.

Xenobombulation

I've got work to do right now, and I really should get on with it, but I'm xenobombulating again. Xenobombulation is the act of avoiding one's duties, malingering, even feigning illness or pulling some stunt like writing a blog post when you really should be getting on with real work.

III

STRANGE WORDS

*"We don't just borrow words; on occasion, English has pur-
sued other languages down alleyways to beat them uncon-
scious and rifle their pockets for new vocabulary."*
~ Booker T. Washington

This book could and should be popular among epeolatrists, dammit! It was written with epeolatrists in
mind. An epeolatrist is, literally, one who worships words,
but if we're to be precise with the definition, worship is a
bit of a stretch. We're really talking about those who like
to expand or test their vocabulary. If you are such a one,
then you might like to chew on these ten words:

Deipnosophy

Last night was definitely a night of deipnosophy, although at points, I'm sad to say, the conversation de-
scended to the realm of political correctness. Americans
are, in my experience, more prone to "politically correct"
word deployment than the British. This is something I
have learned firsthand, being a Brit in America in a house-
hold of Americans. So, last night at dinner, as I observed
(to myself) my dinner companions picking their way
through a minefield of words for the umpteenth time, I
speculated (to myself) whether it would be correct to say
that they live in an epeocratic world—that is, that they are

ruled by words. But not being sure whether *epeocratic* is a word, I never mentioned it.

My instinct was correct. It's not a word, but *deipnosophy* is. Deipnosophy is educated banter or, more accurately, learned dinner conversation. It derives from *deipnon,* the Greek word for *dinner.* Last night, the deipnosophy was taken down a notch by rampant political correctness.

Lethologica

My shameful failure to think of a word that specifically means *being ruled by words* may have been just another example of lethologica—or it may not.

There may not be a single word that precisely means *being ruled by words,* even though, for example, there is *anemocracy,* which means *government by whim,* and there's *beerocracy,* which is *government by brewers,* and there's even *harlotocracy,* which means *government by ladies of the night.* Lethologica, as I'm sure you've realized, is a condition characterized by an inability to find the right word for something.

Thymogenic

The word *thymogenic* emerged in a conversation recently. I observed that almost all American television programs, especially those in prime time, culminate in what I call "The American Moment"—the inevitable, frequently teary, occasionally self-aware, but always sentimental denouement in which hero, heroine and a gaggle of minor characters come together and valiantly resist the urge to dissolve into a group hug. The American Moment is fundamentally thymogenic, the result of thymogenesis.

You might know this word and its forms if you study alternative medicine. The thymus is regarded by some as the center of emotions within the endocrine system.

There's even a *chakra* located there or thereabouts. *Thymogenic* means *generated by emotion*.

I can give you another example. This is a slightly different kind of American Moment. When the conversation turns to Darwinism and evolution in America, the discussion is, or almost always becomes, thymogenic.

Umami

Apparently, the tongue is capable of detecting five distinct classes of taste: sweet, salty, sour, bitter and umami. Although, at the Mexican restaurant last night, I suspect that a sixth taste made a guest appearance: severe jalapeno, a taste situated somewhere between piquant and the fires of hell.

Umami is the taste of meat. And it's a Japanese idea. For most of us, umami is a pleasant, complex taste sensation, a fact that caused me to ponder out loud at dinner whether the animals we eat took a clever Darwinian decision when they chose to be domesticated, if they did.

Fortuitism

Did cows Darwinistically evolve with umami in mind? Did they improve the taste of their flesh so that we would farm them, thus severely diminishing their life expectancy, but rapidly increasing their population? This formulation creates an entertaining paradox, since all the fauna we farm (pigs, cows, sheep, chicken, etc.) exist in much greater populations than they ever would if we were all vegans.

I've always had a bad feeling about Darwinism. I acquired it watching nature programs, where the commentator would proclaim that the brilliant angelfish, for example, had developed its glorious coloring so that it could attract mates. A few moments later, some sandy-colored bottom-feeder would be congratulated for its stunning camouflage, which kept it safe from predators (and rapacious angelfish as well, I shouldn't wonder).

Darwinism is tautological. I prefer the concept of fortuitism: evolution by nothing more than chance variation.

Hylozoist

I'm also a hylozoist—someone who suspects that all matter is endowed with life. Of course, I don't pursue this to the insane conclusion that, for example, my stapler is alive, although it does seems to have a mind of its own at times.

I'm more struck by the fact that when you study the inner doctrines of the more respectable religions, the discussions of the origin of the universe are remarkably similar and equally paradoxical, no matter whether you insert God into the equation or remove Him/Her/It entirely. Hylozoists tend towards the "God conclusion." If the universe is endowed with life then...

Cladogenesis

What I'm saying here is that science and religion appear to be cladogenetic in their theories of creation. They are historically cladogenetic anyway. Cladogenesis is evolution by means of branching off from a common ancestor and I'm using the term metaphorically.

Tetrapyloctomy

Okay, I admit that you can argue that the scientific method and religion have little in common intellectually, but I personally think that's just tetrapyloctomy. For example, Isaac Newton, the father of physics, used the scientific method and, while he was no theologian, he spent a good deal of his later life studying the Torah. He was neither atheist nor agnostic. Tetrapyloctomy? That would be the splitting of hairs four ways.

Ultracrepidate

Of course, we are all prone to ultracrepidation, and to be honest when someone starts to propose "intelligent design" as the genesis of life on this planet, I'm wont to ultracrepidate with the best of them (i.e., to criticize beyond my sphere of knowledge). The problem I have with intelligent design is that it's not really a theory, because it defines no mechanism for evolution. However, that doesn't mean that there is no such God-given mechanism.

Astraphobia

Some people of the religious persuasion with whom I have discussed intelligent design may have hoped that I would be struck down by lightning—especially when I resorted to sarcasm. Maybe they've even prayed for it. If so, they've prayed to the wrong god. Thor (of the Norse pantheon) and Zeus (of the Greek pantheon) are the ones to be beseeched in that regard. In any event, I'm not astrophobic. Them thunderbolts don't scare me.

IV

Short Words

"Therefore, since brevity is the soul of wit, and tediousness the limbs and outward flourishes, I will be brief." ~ Polonius, in William Shakespeare's, *Hamlet*

I didn't feel yare by any means. In fact, I was in a kef as I strolled through the wen. I turned down a ginnel towards the suq, accidentally kicking a tot and uttering a gar. I disturbed a mewing cat. It mowed, but never moved. Lief I began to wonder whether the suq would be zoic. After all, I was hoping to snup a dah from Ali the sutler.

Complete gibberish, right? But all the words are real and all of the unfamiliar ones are short. If you play Scrabble® a good deal, you may know all of these words and even their meanings. But everyone else should be at sea, so let's unravel the paragraph above, word by word.

Yare

I'm not sure why this word isn't used a good bit more. It means *nimble, alert, prepared*. When I hear a sound in the night and I get up to find out what it is, I'm either yare or frightened out of my skin, depending. So, "I didn't feel yare by any means."

Kef

The word *kef* refers to a dreamy state, possibly drug induced. It is quite the opposite of yare. So, "I didn't feel yare by any means, in fact I felt as though I was in a kef."

Wen (and Ginnel and Suq)

A wen can be any of the following four: a sebaceous cyst, a spongy head growth that some goldfish have, a character from the Old English alphabet derived from a rune, and a highly congested city. I think we'll go with *highly congested city* here.

Ginnel. This is a word I heard time and again in Liverpool, but I've not heard it elsewhere. So you may know it. It means *alleyway*.

Suq. You may also be familiar with this word. I know it as *souk*, which is a Middle Eastern market. Suqs are not like normal markets; you bargain for things before you buy them. It's the way it works. The vendors always ask outrageous prices if you aren't prepared to bargain. The correct bargaining strategy in the suk is to feign interest. The first thing you show interest in should not be the thing you want.

Tot

This has multiple meanings, too, most of which you will know. A tot is a small child or a tot is a small amount (of rum, perhaps). You can also use *tot* as a verb, meaning *to add something up*.

Here it means none of those. The word *tot* in our paragraph means *a bone or some other object one might retrieve from a pile of garbage*. (I resent it if you think I would actually kick a small child—or a small amount of rum, for that matter.)

18

Gar

"Shiver me timbers" is a gar. Having one's timbers shiver, by the way, is what happens at sea in wooden ships when the weather is bad and the ships take a battering. It's the old sea dog equivalent of "cross my heart and hope to die"—a mild oath or curse. So "I turned down a ginnel towards the suq, accidentally kicking a tot and uttering a gar."

Mew (and Mow)

The word *mew* does not just describe the noise a cat makes; it can also mean *moulting*. Thus a mewing cat may not be making a sound, as in this instance. To mow is to grimace, when you're not cutting grass. "I disturbed a mewing cat. Lief it mowed, but never moved."

Lief (and Zoic)

Lief means both *soon* and *gladly*. In our opening paragraph it means *soon*.

Zoic. You might just know this one, or be able to work it out. Literally, it means *containing evidence of life*.

"Lief I began to wonder whether the suq would be zoic."

Snup

A suq is a good place to snup. To snup is to buy something of value, which some less discerning person has discarded or sold cheap. Several years ago, I came across an antiques dealer who had had an oil painting—a Constable, no less—snupped from him. The worst part of this experience was that the newspapers and the national media got wind of this event, and, in short order, everyone knew he'd been snupped.

Dah

A dah is a short heavy Burmese knife, often with an ornate ivory handle. It's conceivable that you could find one in a suq.

Sutler

And a sutler is the right kind of person to get a dah from. Believe it or not, a sutler is a camp follower, one who hangs around the army to sell provisions to the soldiers. So, I was hoping to snup a dah from Ali the sutler.

V

VERY LONG WORDS

"I am a bear of very little brain, and long words bother me."
~ Pooh, in A.A. Milne's, *Winnie-the-Pooh*

In choosing to provide a list of long words that you (or at least most of you) don't know, I decided to eschew two very specific words—*antidisestablishmentarianism* and *floccinaucinihilipilification*—my presumption being that you will have run into both of them. When I was at school, I was unreliably informed that the longest English word was the first of these two, and later, when I went to university, I was unreliably corrected when told that the longest English word was in fact the second of these two.

Antidisestablishmentarianism has 28 letters and can be blamed on the marital difficulties of Henry VIII, who, when forbidden to get a divorce by Pope Clement VII, set himself up as "Pope of the English Church," thus inconveniently linking the English church directly to the state. By the 19th century, some British politicians had begun to conclude that this linkage was a bad idea (suffering perhaps from America envy) and they became known as disestablishmentarians. Naturally, other politicians opposed this and thus talked-the-talk as antidisestablishmentarians.

In the length race, *floccinaucinihilipilification* noses ahead of *antidisestablishmentarianism* by a single letter and it is a lot easier to define. It means the *categorization of something as worthless trivia*. For example, my definition of *antidisestablishmentarianism* could, and probably should, be floccinaucinihilipilificated.

The movie, *Mary Poppins*, put both of these words into the shade with the song titled, "Supercalifragilisticexpialidocious," which is a word of 34 letters. Technically this is a nonsense word, but if you believe the words of the song, this is a word that is properly used only if you can't think of anything to say. Thus, it is always used improperly, since, if you can't think of some thing to say and you think to use this word, then you can think of something to say and, hence, shouldn't say it.

Pseudoantidisestablishmentarianism

Let's face it; this word is just a cheat. Technically, of course, it means *a feigned opposition to the separation of the state from the Church*, and at 34 letters it draws level with the Mary Poppins nonsense. But, if we're going to play fast and loose with the prefixes, why not *pseudofloccinaucinihilipilification*—feigning to categorize something as worthless trivia? Or *pseudosupercalifragilisticexpialidocious*—a word you say when you actually can think of something to say, but want to give the impression that you can't think of something to say?

Hippopotomonstrosesquippediliophobia

This word is blatantly intimidating and was almost certainly invented by a sadistic psychiatrist. At 36 letters, it's longer than any of the words mentioned above and it means (I almost can't believe it) *the fear of long words*. Only a sadistic psychiatrist would concoct such a word to describe the fear of such long words. I mean, how is that preferable to *longwordophobia*?

Circumbilivagination

I knew I would have to include some relatively short words, and at 20 letters this one is somewhat hippopoto-monstrosesquippediliophobically challenged. *Circumbili-vagination* means *to move in a circle or walk around*. There is a plethora of words that have the same or a similar meaning: to circle, to orbit, to wheel, to whirl, to circuit, to rotate, to revolve, to circumambulate, to circumgyrate and to circumnavigate. That's why *circumbilivagination* rarely comes up in conversation.

Honorificabilitudinitatibus

This is a Shakespearean contribution, in the sense that Shakespeare is purported to have spoiled some perfectly good paper with this word. It means *the state of being able to achieve honors*. Presumably just before the 2008 Beijing Olympics, Michael Phelps was honorificabilitudinitatibic. To be honest, I'm not sure whether Shakespeare used this word in a play, a sonnet, or a blog posting.

Cholangiocholecystocholedochectomy

I have my doubts that this word qualifies as a genuine long word. It has 34 letters and it refers to a medical procedure that involves cutting out the hepatic duct, the common bile duct, and the gall bladder. I really don't believe this word ever gets used in conversations with surgeons. I say that because my uncle was a heart surgeon and I never heard him use it.

Having now listed 5 words, I think it's time to state some of the principles I'm applying here. I really do believe that some words can't be counted as long words if they are too specialized, so the last one doesn't really count. I mean, I could have thrown in *pneumonoultrami-croscopicsilicovolcanoconiosis* (45 letters), which is *a coal-*

mining disease of the lungs, but that doesn't meet the standard. There are probably shed-loads of chemical names that stretch "to infinity and beyond" that would vote themselves onto this list if I let them.

I'm also excluding place names and their derivatives (Liverpudlian, Mancunian, etc.), but I may as well mention, en passant, that *Chargoggagoggmanchauggagoggchaubunagungamaugg* is the longest U.S. place name. It has been attached to a lake in Webster, Maine. The name is a Nipmuk (American Indian) word and denotes a local agreement between the Nipmuks and neighboring tribes—the Narraganssett, Pequot and Mohegan. It means, *"You fish on the left side; I'll fish on the right side; no one fishes in the middle."* Presumably, an ancestor of Dr. Henry Kissinger brokered that agreement.

I have traveled much of North Wales and I never once encountered a whirlpool or a red cave for that matter. However, I suppose I might have if only I'd visited the village with the U.K.'s longest name: *Llanfairpwllgwyngyllgogerychwyrndrobwllllantysiliogogogoch*. It means, *"St. Mary's Church in the hollow of the white hazel near to the rapid whirlpool of Llantysilio of the Red Cave."*

Proceeding on:

Entredentolignumologist

This is one of those words where you feel you just might be able to work out the meaning. But you can't and you won't.

It refers to a person who collects toothpick boxes. The remarkable thing here is that, search as I might, I can't find a word for someone who collects toothpicks and yet there's a word for someone who collects the boxes they come in?

Aichmorhabdophobia (and Bathysiderodromophobia)

The first of these words presents a similar conundrum to *entredentolignumologist*. *Aichmorhabdophobia* refers to the fear of being beaten with a pointed stick. However, there is no corresponding word for the fear of being beaten with a blunt stick, or a thin stick, or any other kind of stick. It's a word with no relatives—a kind of orphaned stick phobia.

Inventing new phobias is a good way to concoct new long words, and when I came across *bathysiderodromophobia*, which is an overlong word for the fear of subways, it occurred to me to cross-breed this with *aichmorhabdophobia*, to give *aichmorhabdobathysiderodromophobia*. I could then pretend that this was the fear of being beaten with a pointed stick in a subway. That would have been an impressive 34 letters, but *hippopotomonstrosesquippedaliophobia* would still be longer, so I resisted the temptation.

Gynotikolobomassophile

This describes someone who likes to nibble on a woman's earlobe. I guess it's a stage that all us men have to go through a few years after our voices break. There is no equivalent word to describe someone who likes to nibble on the male earlobe, which seems an oversight because I personally know someone who does.

Aequeosalinocalcalinosetaceoaluminosocupreovitriolic

And if you've visited Bath, then you'll know exactly what I mean. It's an accurate *description of the spa waters at Bath* and clocks in at a whopping 52 letters. The word, coined by Edward Strother (1635-1737), to describe those

25

waters, is often used by visitors to that wonderful spa town thusly:

"Darling, shall we take the waters this morning."

"Oh, yes dear, they're so aequeosalinocalcalinoseta-ceoaluminosocupreovitriolic."

This word, incidentally, may qualify as the longest in the English language. Or it may not.

Lopadotemachoselachogaleokranioleipsanodrim-hypotrimmatosilphioparaomelitokatakechymeno-kichlepikossyphophattoperisteralektryonoptekephal-liokigklopeleiolagoiosiraiobaphetraganopterygon

If *supercalifragilisticexpialidocious*, concocted by P. L. Travers, qualifies for the long word contest, then surely words concocted by Aristophanes qualify, too. In which case, *lopadotemachoselachogaleokranioleipsanodrimhypotrim-matosilphioparaomelitokatakechymenokichlepikossyphophatto-peristeralektryonoptekephalliokigklopeleiolagoiosiraiobaphetra-ganopterygon*, with 182 letters, wins the contest. It would also be a good word to use as a tie-breaker in a spelling bee.

This gargantuan word means: *a ghoulash composed of all the leftovers from the meals of the last two weeks*.

Admittedly this is very, very long for a word, but actually, it's reasonably concise as a recipe.

VI

Useful Words

"One forgets words as one forgets names. One's vocabulary needs constant fertilizing or it will die." ~ Evelyn Waugh

Just as there are some words that don't serve any useful purpose, there are some words that you've probably never run into that are really useful, or at least it feels quite satisfying that such a word exists, because you can see the need for it. The following is a list of words that I am, definitely, in favor of. I hope you will use them whenever the occasion arises.

Loganamnosis

We particularly advocate the frequent use of this word, since we suffer from this condition ourselves and we're pretty sure that many people suffer in the same way. Loganamnosis occurs when we're talking about something and, well, we just can't pluck the right word out of our memory. *Loganamnosis* doesn't actually mean *not being able to remember a word*. It refers to the obsession we develop, which has us focusing on trying to remember the damn word we couldn't quite retrieve and stops us from giving our attention to the conversation.

We may even blather on after the fashion of "What was that word? It begins with an *o*. Or maybe a *u*." We're even likely to burst into the conversation a few minutes later and say, "We remember now! The word is *loganamnosis*!" And just in case loganamnosis really does cause logan-amnosis in us, there's an easier word to remember that means something similar: Onomatomania is our extreme vexation at having difficulty finding the right word.

Nosism

You may have noticed that the description of *loganamnosis* reads a little oddly. That's because it was carried out in the first person plural. I was practicing nosism. Only a nosist would write in that way, because nosism is the practice of referring to oneself as "we."

This is something for which Queen Victoria became famous when she declared, "We are not amused," instead of using the more familiar, "Curl up and die, you little toad." There is something quite pompous about the use of the first person plural in this way, since it presumes agreement by everyone present.

A word closely related to nosism is *wegotism*. The meaning is slightly different since *wegotism* refers to the excessive use of *we* in writing (but not in speech). We can thus proclaim that our description of *loganamnosis* was both wegotistical and nosistical.

Culacino

My eyes lit up when I encountered this word, partly because I'm utterly useless with coasters. When I want to put a drink down on a surface, nothing in me says, "You must get a coaster to put it on." When I've put an inconvenient stain on a table surface, I think, "Why can't they invent surfaces that don't stain?" But if it weren't for people like me, there would be no need for the word *culacino*. A culacino (probably pronounced ku-l*uh*-*ch*ee-noh, because of its Italian origin) is the mark left on a table by a moist glass, put there by some inconsiderate, lazy so-and-so who couldn't be bothered to use a coaster.

Lubberland

When I die I hope to go to Lubberland, where I will surely meet other poor souls who, in their lifetimes, left plenty of culacinos on tables, nightstands and assorted pieces of furniture. You see, in Lubberland, the culacinos never form on the furniture, the dishes never pile up in the sink, and the garbage puts itself out to be collected. Lubberland is a place inhabited by the kind of people who work at the desk next to yours, but who send you emails because they can't be bothered to stand up and engage you in conversation.

Lubberland's inhabitants are those who would spend hours driving around parking lots looking for a space close to the shop they want to visit, because walking will surely exhaust them. But in Lubberland—hallelujah!—there's always a parking space waiting for you. Lubberlanders have remote controls for their remote controls and, if they lose the remote for the remote, no worries! They have a remote for the remote for the remote. In short, Lubberland is a mythical paradise reserved for those who are lazier than a pillow tester and mean to remain so.

Lubberland! Where seldom is heard a discouraging word and effort has vanished away.

Grinagog

Should I die and find myself in Lubberland, I would soon be grinning like the cat's uncle. I would undoubtedly become a grinagog, a person who is perpetually grinning. *Grinagog* is, to my mind, a wonderful word, because it is almost onomatopoeic and much better than *grizzledemundy*, which means exactly the same, but fails to telegraph the meaning. In fact, if I had to wager, I would have bet that it meant the exact opposite.

Eccedentesiast

I would not become an eccedentesiast, the eccedentesiast being the opposite of a grinagog. The grinagog may be a bit of a simpleton, but he is smiling because he (or she) is somehow amused or happy. The eccedentesiast is the one faking the smile. The word was coined by Florence King, the so-called "Queen of Mean," who penned a column called "The Misanthrope's Corner" in the U.S. magazine, *National Review*. She was particularly referring to those who brandish fake smiles for the television camera, which, to me, means quiz show hosts and politicians.

Macrologist

Of course, if you run into a macrologist, it's possible that you will become an eccedentesiast for the sake of politeness. A macrologist is a boring conversationalist, the kind of person who, as Henry Ford once said, "opens his mouth and puts his feats in it."

This is an odd word which seems as inappropriate to its meaning as *grinagog* is appropriate. The origin of the word is from the Greek *macrologia*, which simply means *a long discourse* (a lot of words), with no specific implication of boredom. However, bores and long discourses are often intimate friends.

The worst thing about a bore is not so much that they won't stop talking, but that they won't let you stop listening. They provoke you into drinking quickly so that you can escape from them in order to refill your glass. After all, you can only play the eccedentesiast for so long. As George Eliot said, "Blessed is the man who, having nothing to say, refrains from giving wordy evidence of the fact."

Vilipend

Thomas Aldrich noted that, "The man who suspects his own tediousness has yet to be born," and yet, we have no difficulty recognizing tediousness in others and vilipending them for it. For that reason, champion bores are often vilipended.

Take, for instance, the case of Herbert Tree, who vilipended one putative bore by saying, "He is an old bore; even the grave yawns for him."

You've probably figured out that to vilipend is to disparage or belittle others. Vilipending is an art unto itself, with many practitioners, but few artists.

Former U.K. Labour Minister, Denis Healey, ranks among the great vilipenders of all time for his comment about Parliamentary opponent, Sir Geoffrey Howe. Healey remarked that, "Being attacked by Sir Geoffrey is like being mauled by a dead sheep."

Mamie Van Doren was no slouch, either, in the vilipending department. She crucified Warren Beatty's ego with the words, "He's the type of man who will end up dying in his own arms." She thus achieved in a single sentence what Carly Simon took a whole song—"You're So Vain"—to accomplish.

Johnny Mercer, though, is the *victor vilipendorum* for his curt dismissal of a particular British West End musical: "I could eat alphabet soup and shit better lyrics."

Garbist

Vilipending might be great fun if you happen to have a lively wit and a sharp tongue, but it can be a dangerous pursuit. As Richard Steele observed, "Nothing can atone for the lack of modesty, without which beauty is ungraceful and wit detestable."

A garbist is, if nothing else, modest. The word refers to someone who is adept at engaging in polite behavior.

31

The word seems to be a little schizophrenic, because on the one hand there is *garbage*, which derives from the Old French word *jarbage*, meaning *a bundle of sheaves or entrails*. On the other hand there is the word *garb*, which originally meant *elegance*, from the French *garbe* and the Italian *garbo* (making Greta Garbo's name seem somewhat appropriate). The garbist is, thus, elegant in behavior.

Denary

My lists of obscure words come in tens. As I've said elsewhere in this book, there's a reason for this: people like lists of ten things. That's why David Letterman of the Late Show regularly produces "Top Ten" lists, a tradition that, bizarrely, began on his show with "The Top Ten Things that Almost Rhyme with Peas," but normally coincides with what's in the news. In the 2008 U.S. election, for example, Letterman did "The Top Ten Questions People Are Asking the John McCain Campaign," "The Top Ten Surprising Things about Obama," and "The Top Ten Messages on Sarah Palin's Answering Machine." In the U.K., *The Sun* newspaper is forever publishing lists of ten.

I'm simply playing the same tune on a different instrument. The number *10* is, as we all know, the default number of fingers on our hands and the basis of our counting system. Ten is also the Pythagorean symbol (number) for completeness, because 1 plus 2 plus 3 plus 4 equals 10. The number of commandments in The Old Testament? Ten, of course. And if you want to get even more biblical, there were ten generations between Adam and Noah, and ten horns on the Beast of Revelation.

In any event, all of these things are decads (groups of ten things), and all my lists are denary (consisting of ten parts). You've got to give people what they want, right?

VII

WORDS THAT SHOULDN'T EXIST

"What is required is not a lot of words, but effectual ones."
~ Seneca

Some words shouldn't exist because there is no logical sense in their existence. All the words I describe here exist. I found them in reputable reference areas on the web or in dictionaries. Nevertheless, they are all ridiculous and unnecessary. I humbly propose that we rid ourselves of these words. Let's face it; you've never met with these words before. So how much of a tragedy would it be if you never meet with them again? And if by some slim chance you actually have already met with some of these words, I'm sure you'll be happy for them to disappear from our existence anyway. Here's my list of the superfluous:

Poodle-faker

A poodle-faker is a young man who seeks advancement through his association with female society and particularly with wealthy women. The term derives from the use of the term *poodle*, which was a slang term for a woman in the U.K. at the beginning of the 20th century, and *faking*, since the man's interest is on the money or professional advancement, not the woman.

No matter. That time has gone and this word can happily be put to rest. The word *gigolo* is perfectly adequate for describing men who trade their charms for wealth through their association with women.

Phobologophobia

There are lots of phobia words I have a problem with. I really don't like *porphyrophobia*—the fear of the color purple—not because people have no right to have a fear of a given color, but because there is no corresponding word for fears of other colors in the spectrum, like green, red or blue. I'm not particularly partial to *ornithoscelida-phobia*, the fear of dinosaurs. First of all, there aren't any around so being afraid of them makes no sense. But even if you allow that phobias are products of the imagination to some degree, then it's simply unfair that there is a word for the fear of reptiles from the Mesozoic era, but no words for extinct classes of fauna from other periods. Nevertheless, if we're going to lose a phobia word, let's lose *phobologophobia*, the fear of words about fears. How does that make any sense at all?

Ascian

An ascian is a person (or thing) that has no shadow. The word is connected with the fact that, in the tropics when the sun is exactly overhead, people don't cast much of a shadow. But, and I'm going to be completely pedantic here, they do cast a shadow. Even if they didn't (but they do), they would only *not* cast a shadow for a very short time in the day, and then only on one day of the year when the sun was precisely overhead. So when would anyone ever use this word? The reason for its existence is thinner than the shadow cast by an ascian stick insect.

Pentapopemptic

If you've been divorced two, three, four or six times, there's no simple word to describe you. But if you've been divorced five times, there is. It's pentapopemptic and it's superfluous.

Furr-ahin (and Fittie-lan)

I can't remember which word is which, but according to my research, one of these two refers to "the hindmost horse on the right pulling a plough," and the other to "the near horse of the hindmost pair pulling a plough."

The way I read that, the furr-ahin can also be the fittie-lan and, since no one uses horse-pulled ploughs anymore (Americans call them *plows*), there's no one to consult about it. Neither can we discover whether there is a word among the ploughmen for the hindmost horse on the left or the far horse of the hindmost pair. But there's no reason to know, anyway.

No matter how charitable we want to be, it's pretty much over for these words. Let's consign them to some rural word museum somewhere and be done with it.

Mallemaroking

This is another gradually dying word. You can blame *The Chambers Dictionary* for that, although you can also blame *Chambers* for keeping it alive. *Mallemaroking* is believed to derive from the Dutch *mallemerok*, which refers to a romping woman or possibly a tomboy. The word means *the carousing of seamen in icebound Greenland whaling ships*.

Okay, I am not a whaler and never have been, so I'm not really sure what such carousing involves or even why it takes place, except for the obvious explanation that if there's no whaling to be done, and you are locked in by ice, then you may as well carouse a little. However, the definition of the word is gradually being amputated.

Over time it seems to have lost its Greenland aspect and its whaling aspect, so that, in the latest edition of *Chambers,* it is simply the kind of thing that seamen do on icebound ships.

My guess is that *Chambers* is desperately trying to save this word by making it more general. But really, ships don't get icebound much anymore, so if we're going to save this word then more cutting is required. I humbly suggest *mallemaroking: the carousing of seamen.* I make this suggestion because I'm convinced that seamen can be depended upon to carouse at some time or other.

Alternatively, let's forget the damn word.

Zygopleural

I object to the word *zygopleural* because *zygomorphic* also exists and means exactly the same thing: *having bilateral symmetry.* Neither of these words sees a great deal of use because most people are not exactly sure what bilateral symmetry is. One of them should gracefully step aside for the benefit of the other. My choice for the shredder is *zygopleural.*

Abacinate

To abacinate means *to blind someone,* but more than that, *to blind them by putting a hot copper basin near their eyes.* I have two problems with this word. First, blinding someone is not nice and we shouldn't have too many words to describe such behavior. The second problem I have is, it's far too specific. Such specialization in a word is unnecessary and it should be retired accordingly. Get rid of the word; get rid of the behavior, I say.

Zumbooruk

I have no idea whether it is possible to fire a cannon that is being carried on the back of a camel. My guess is that it is, indeed, possible—if the cannon isn't too large. But my guess is based entirely on the fact that the word *zumbooruk* exists at all and purportedly refers to a cannon fired from the back of a camel.

Unfortunately, no one is sure how to spell the word; *zumbooruck, zomboruk, zamboorak, zamburak* and *zamburek* are all equally valid, and the operator of the cannon can be referred to either as a *zumboorukchee* or a *zamburakchi*.

This is all completely hopeless. How can you have a word with so many spellings? It would be a nightmare at a spelling bee. Who would dare to say that any spelling was actually wrong? No one does cannons on camels anymore, and even when they did, no one was sure how to spell the damn word. We can surely let this one go.

Xenoglossy

This is a complete self-contradiction. Xenoglossy is the ability to speak a language without having learned it. You heard me. I simply don't believe it's possible to start spontaneously spouting off fluently in an unfamiliar language. Hence, there is no point in having a word for an ability that doesn't exist.

If you ever run into someone who claims to be capable of speaking a language without ever learning it, send this person to me and I'll happily shoot the faker.

VIII

Words You Didn't Know Were Eponyms

*"I once had a rose named after me and I was very flattered.
But I was not pleased to read the description in the catalogue:
no good in a bed, but fine up against a wall."*
~ Eleanor Roosevelt

Pyrrhic is an odd word—an adjective that only ever describes one noun: *victory*. It is an eponym, as you probably know, referring to Pyrrhus of Epirus. Pyrrhus, a Greek king, fought the Romans on several occasions, most famously at the battle of Asculum. He won the battle, but at the cost of 3,500 dead. No matter that 6,000 Romans also died on the field; Pyrrhus was heard to say after the battle that he could not afford another such victory.

The English language contains many eponyms. An eponym is the name of an object, institution, place, activity, or whatever, that is derived from a person's name or that of a product. Many eponyms are "proprietary eponyms"—Xerox, Hoover, Aspirin, Kleenex and Google, for example—brands or trademarks that have, since their invention or creation, entered the language as common nouns, verbs or adjectives.

To my knowledge there's only one *half*-eponym. It is *gerrymander*, the portmanteau word (see Section XVIII) combining *Gerry* (after American politician and Governor of Massachusetts, Elbridge Gerry, 1744-1814) and *salamander* (as in amphibian). The term refers to fixing an election by fixing the boundaries of the voting area so that it includes a high percentage of people who are likely to vote for you. The voting district foisted on Massachusetts by Elbridge Gerry gave rise to an area shaped like a salamander.

In many cases we may know the origin of an eponym, or at least we sense that the word is an eponym even if we're not exactly sure who or what has given the word its name. We'd probably suspect that *maverick* was an eponym, for example, even if we didn't know anything of Samuel Augustus Maverick, the American pioneer rancher who never put his brand on his cattle.

What I've tried to assemble here is a list of surprising eponyms:

Panic

This word derives directly from the Greek god, Pan, whose domain was nature, fertility, the woods, shepherds and the flocks they minded. Pan liked to party. He spent a good deal of time dancing with nymphs and playing on his pipes. Nevertheless, he was dreaded and feared by those who traveled through the woods by night. Sudden fright without any visible cause was ascribed to Pan, giving us the word *panic*.

There are many other eponyms from Ancient Greece, including: morphine (from Morpheus, Greek god of dreams), erotic (from Eros, Greek god of love), tantalize (from Tantalus, mythical king of Phrygia), and lesbian (from the Greek poetess, Sappho of Lesbos).

From the Roman, we get: volcano and vulcanize (from Vulcan, god of fire), fauna (from Faunus, god of pastures), flora (from Flora, goddess of flowers) and venereal (from Venus, goddess of love).

Lynch

There's genuine competition for this word, as there are many possible originators. We can start with James Fitz-stephen Lynch, mayor of Galway in 1493, who hanged his own son for killing the nephew of a Spanish friend—an action that displeased the people of Galway. Lynch may have been his name, but technically that wasn't a lynch-ing, just a common or garden hanging, so his claim to eponymity is thin.

There was an Englishman named Lynch, who was sent to the colonies in 1687 to deal with piracy. Not be-ing much of a bureaucrat, Lynch had a habit of hanging pirates without the rigmarole of a trial.

Then there was that unfortunate incident near Lynch Creek in Franklin County, North Carolina (around 1778), when Major Beard, a Tory, was hanged by a group of American patriots led by Major John Drake. Lynch Creek was surely named after some Lynch or other, but no one is sure which one, so there's no direct claim to the eponym in this instance. Nevertheless, we know that a lynching—a hanging without trial—took place there once.

There was also the Virginian magistrate, Charles Lynch (1736-96), who presided over an informal court during the American Revolution and, last but not least, there is William Lynch (1742-1820), a Virginian plantation owner and vigilante, who was reportedly keen on dispensing justice with a noose.

So many lynchings and so many Lynches clamoring for eponymity...

Nicotine

Nicotine is an alkaloid found in tobacco leaves, which is primarily responsible for the common addiction to cig-arettes. Tobacco—as we all know—was first brought to Europe by Sir Walter Raleigh in 1586 from the Colonies, part of which Raleigh named *Virginia* after the "Virgin Queen," Elizabeth I.

But in truth, that isn't the truth. Tobacco came to Europe well ahead of Raleigh's adventures. Jean Nicot was the French ambassador to Portugal, residing in Lisbon from 1559 to 1561. He was sent there to arrange the marriage of six-year-old Princess Marguerite de Valois to five-year-old King Sebastian of Portugal, and when he returned he brought tobacco seeds and powdered leaves to France. He introduced snuff to the French court, and the substance immediately gained the favor of Catherine de Medici, the French *reine du jour*. The *fashionistas* of the day took to the drug, which made Nicot a celebrity. That caused the tobacco plant to be named *nicotiana tabacum* after Nicot, and the alkaloid to be named for the plant.

Zany

This word comes directly from *Zanni*, which is an Italian nickname for *Giovanni*, the Italian version of the English name, *John*. It connects directly to the Commedia dell'arte, a kind of street theater that was popular in Italy from the 16th to 18th century. *Zanni* is the name of one of the comedic characters (a servant) of the Commedia dell'arte, but the name is also used collectively to describe all the characters, which include: Arlechino (the Harlequin), Pedrolino (the Pierrot), Il Capitano (the Captain), Pulcinella (Punch), Colombina, Sacaramuccia (or Scaramouche) and Pantalone.

Zanni by name; zany by nature.

Dunce

How are the mighty fallen! The eminent John Duns Scotus (1266-1308) is deemed to be among the most important theologians and philosophers of the High Middle Ages. He was even nicknamed *Doctor Subtilis*, in celebration of his brilliant and nuanced manner of thought, which culminated in the theological doctrine known as Scotism. But his work was not so highly prized by the philosophers of the 16th century, who accused him of sophistry. Eventually, the word *dunce*, a corruption of his middle name, came to denote *someone incapable of scholarship*, and the conical, comical dunce cap—worn by pupils who disrupted classrooms—was invented. So John Duns Scotus became eponymous twice: once for his brilliance in founding Scotism, and again for his lack of brillance in being the original dunce.

Silhouette

A silhouette is the shadow cast by the outline of an object, at least that's how we use the word nowadays. That's because we now have cameras. Before the camera existed, one way of recording a person's image (after a fashion) was to cut his profile into a card—usually a dark card. Such images were known as silhouettes, named for Etienne de Silhouette (1709-1767), a French finance minister who was no great shakes as an economist, but a whiz with a pair of scissors.

Salmonella

Theobald Smith (1859-1934) is best remembered for his work on anaphylaxis, the acquired hypersensitivity against proteins. That's hardly fair. He also discovered salmonella, which is a hog cholera bacillus. During the study of hog cholera, which was done together with American veterinary surgeon, Elmer Salmon (1850-1914), Smith made the dramatic discovery that dead bacteria would still provoke an immune system response. Thus, it would be possible to immunize animals against living bacteria using dead bacteria. This discovery became the foundation for the development of a typhus vaccine and, later, Jonas Salk's polio vaccine. Elmer Salmon, being the senior of the two, was able to ensure that he was credited with much of the work that was done by Theobald Smith. Hence, it was Salmon who gave his name to salmonella, which by rights should be called *smithella*.

Comma

It's nice to hark back to a time when people took punctuation seriously. That was certainly the case when Domenico de Comma invented the comma, a punctuation mark that he hoped would make the Bible more accessible and understandable to the reader. Unfortunately, the gentlemen of the Inquisition failed to agree with his bold innovation.

One can only imagine the spirited debate that must have taken place between them: "This house believes that the comma is heresy and an affront to God!"

First the debate, then the auto-da-fé.

Algorithm

Prior to the proliferation of computers, few people outside the field of mathematics knew or cared to know what an algorithm was. (It's an explicit method for solving a problem or doing something useful.)

When software companies started to patent the use of algorithms to carry out specific functions, the word slipped into more common usage, because an algorithm was suddenly something that might make you rich.

Then, when CBS introduced the TV series "Numb3rs" in 2005, everyone got to hear the word—at least once per episode. That's because the series is based on the absurd notion that a make-believe math professor, Charlie Epps, can solve crimes that stump his brother, make-believe FBI agent, Don Epps, by dreaming up mathematical algorithms that somehow have a bearing on the case.

I expect that Abu Abdullah Muhammad bin Musa al-Khwarizmi would have been horrified by the TV show. His name means *person from Khwarizm*—a state that most closely approximates to modern-day Uzbekistan. He was a real-life mathematician in Baghdad and is considered the founder of modern-day algebra. His name was translated into Latin as *Algoritmi,* from which we get the word *algorithm.*

Wisteria

The wisteria is a genus much beloved by English gardeners as a woody vine, with pendulous clusters of flowers, that can climb up the side of a building and fan out in all directions. It is native to America, China, Korea and Japan.

It's possible that it should be written *wistaria,* and that its official spelling is simply an error. If so, Thomas Nuttall made the error. He was a botanist and an admirer of the noted American physician and anatomist, Caspar Wistar, whose life achievements include publishing the two-volume work, *A System of Anatomy,* and developing a means of preserving human remains by injecting them with wax. The wax idea might not seem like such a big deal now, but in the 19th century it was difficult to teach medicine without having preserved specimens to pore over.

So Nuttall misnamed the wisteria after Casper Wistar—or possibly not, because an alternative theory suggests that the genus was named after the notable Quaker, Daniel Wister.

This leaves me with a few words that never made it onto the list of ten, either because they were too well known or because the story behind them never sparked my interest. It's likely that some of these will also be a surprise to you:

- Bigot – a person with pronounced prejudices. Eponym: Nathaniel Bigot (1575-1660), an intolerant English Puritan teacher.

- Bluetooth – the wireless protocol. Eponym: Harald Blatand (c. 910-987), Viking king, whose name translates as *Bluetooth*.

- Bloomers – women's underwear. Eponym: Amelia Jenkins Bloomer (1818-94), American feminist, who never invented but did advocate the wearing of bloomers.

- Diesel – a type of engine, a fossil fuel. Eponym: Rudolf Diesel (1858-1913), German mechanical engineer who designed and built the first diesel engine.

- Doggerel – crude verse with irregular rhythm, bad poetry, often humorous. Eponym: Matthew Doggerel (1330-1405), English poet, who had some unappreciated poems published by Chaucer.

- Hooligan – thief, ruffian. Eponym: Patrick Hooligan, 19th century London-based Irish criminal, thief and ruffian.

- Marmalade – a clear, jellylike preserve made from the pulp and rind of fruits, usually citrus. Eponym: Joao Marmalado from Portugal (1450-1510), who learned to boil oranges with sugar and water.

- Syphilis – venereal disease. Eponym: a character in the poem "Syphilis sive Morbus Gallicus" by Girolamo Fracastro (1483-1553), both the name of a shepherd and the disease he suffered from.

IX

WORDS WHOSE ETYMOLOGY
YOU DON'T KNOW

*"But names, once they are in common use, quickly become
mere sounds, their etymology being buried, like so many of the
earth's marvels, beneath the dust of habit."*
~ Salman Rushdie

I like etymology—the study of the origin of words. It's
enlightening, amusing and confusing all at once. I en-
joy the fact that in the heyday of Communism there were
etymological Marxist theories that sought to prove that
all human language originated from the word *hand*, im-
plying that "the worker" was the foundation of everything, including thought. Did anyone really believe that?
Apparently.

I'm intrigued by what etymology reveals. Consider, for
example, the etymology of the word *sin*. It comes from the
Old English *synn*, which has the meaning of *a crime* and
is associated with doing evil. The Old Norse is *synd*, and
the German *Sünde*. But its inclusion in the Bible is as a
translation from the Latin *peccatum*, which doesn't mean
the same thing at all; its meaning is more along the lines
of *a religious error*.

In the original Greek version of the New Testament,
the word is *hamartia*, which literally means *to miss the target*—a word normally associated with archery. In biblical

Hebrew, the generic word for sin is *het*. It means *to err, to miss the mark*. Judaism teaches that sin is an act, and not a state of being, while Christianity (at some point) decided we were all born in a state of sin. All of which indicates that it's easy for meaning to get mangled in translation.

Here's my list of ten etymological derivations that you are unlikely to know. It's just possible that knowing one or two of these will make you wiser.

Sophisticated

This is a word whose meaning has traveled a great distance. *Sophos* is Greek for *wisdom*; add the word *philos* and we get *philosophy*, the *love of wisdom*. But *sophos* also gives us the word *sophistry*, which refers to deceitful and misleading argument.

The confusion harks back to a division in Ancient Greece between the philosophers (the good guys) and the sophists (the bad guys—despite the fact that *sophos* also means *sage*). The sophists decided to accept money as a fee for enlightening and educating their clients, while the philosophers refused to do so. Eventually the sophists became disingenuous, telling people what they wanted to hear.

So the word *sophisticated* came to mean *deceitful and actively misleading*. That tide turned in the late 19th century when the original Greek root began to reassert itself—probably as a result of academic musings. Soon, no less an authority than the *Oxford English Dictionary* defined a sophisticate as a *person free of naivety*. By 1945 the word sophisticated had acquired the meaning of *being technically superior*.

Salary (and Salient)

The word *salary* comes from the Latin word for salt, which is *sal*. Specifically, it comes from the Latin term *salarium argentum*, which means *money of salt*. In Roman times, salt was used as a currency for practical reasons: it was needed for preserving food and was also useful medicinally as an antiseptic. That made it a commodity that had value in every part of the Roman Empire. Salt was also a commodity whose trade was closely controlled by Rome, and, hence, it became a very convenient and common means of paying the various Roman garrisons that peppered the Roman Empire.

Consequently, you might be inclined to think that the word *salient* (meaning *important*) has the same etymology. Not so, I'm afraid. *Salient* does come from a Latin word, but its root is *salire* (to jump), not *sal*. The meaning of *salient* is, thus, *something that jumps out*.

Punch

In English, the word *punch* has three separate definitions: *to punch a hole in something, to punch someone (especially with the fist),* and *a mixed drink usually containing alcohol.*

The first two meanings come from the Old French noun *ponchon* (a pointed tool), and the verb *ponchonner* (to punch).

I had always thought that the third meaning here derived from the other two, based on the idea of the drink "packing a punch." My experience of drinking some particularly lethal punches at various parties instilled this entirely inaccurate theory in my mind for decades.

The truth is that *punch* (the mixed drink) comes from the Hindi word *paantsch*, which means *five*. A Hindi *paantsch* has five ingredients: spirit, sugar, lemon, water or tea, and spices.

The sailors and employees of the British East India Company brought the drink back from India to England in the early 17th century. Just to confuse the picture, there's *Punsch* (also known as punch), a traditional liqueur of Sweden.

Quarantine

The number *forty* is biblical, very biblical. Noah's Flood lasted 40 days; Moses was 40 years old when called by God; Moses kept the herd of Jethro for 40 years; he stayed for 40 days and 40 nights on the summit of Mount Sinai while the tablets of law were chiseled out. The Hebrews wandered 40 years in the desert. David reigned over Israel for 40 years and Solomon reigned in Jerusalem for 40 years. Forty days after his birth, Jesus was presented to the Temple of Jerusalem. He fasted 40 days in the desert, and 40 days separated his Ascension and his Resurrection. And that's only some of it.

Possibly because 40 is such a popular biblical number, the Venetians decided that it was the right number of days to keep a ship waiting outside the port if it was suspected of carrying disease onboard. When a ship was thought to be infected with disease, the crew and passengers were not permitted to go ashore for 40 days. The Venetians called this restriction period a *quaranténa*, which meant *a period of 40 days*—the word being based on the French word *quarantaine*. This French word, in turn, was derived from the Latin *quadraginta*, meaning *40*. It was the Italian word that was taken into English as *quarantine* in the 17th century.

Dog

I have no doubt that you don't know the etymology of this word, because as far as I can tell nobody does. The same is true, incidentally of the Spanish word for dog, which is *perro*. You'll find *dogge* in Middle English and *dogca* in Old English, but all other IndoEuropean languages have words either like *hund* in German, or like *chien* in French. The latter derives from the Latin *canis*.

Surprisingly, the etymology of the word *canary* also comes from the Latin for dog. Here's how it happened:

When first discovered by the Romans, the island now known as Gran Canaria was called *Insula Canaria*—meaning *island of dogs*. Actually, even though it was inhabited, it is unlikely that there were any dogs there at all. Most likely the Romans were referring to monk seals, which they called sea dogs, rather than real dogs.

When the Spanish took over, they took their cue from the Romans and called the whole group of islands *Islas Canarias*, promptly giving it a coat of arms with two dogs on it.

And so it follows that, when yellow finches were discovered on the islands, they were called *canaries*.

Stork

As a child I would frequently ask my mother where I came from. I probably drove her half mad with the question. She usually told me that the stork brought me—a fact that she tried to confirm at some point by taking me to see Walt Disney's animated movie, *Dumbo*. I didn't believe a word of it, of course.

Nevertheless, mothers all across Europe and America perpetuate the myth of an army of storks carrying babies—bundled in white cloth—in their beaks. There's even a superstition in some areas that a stork can cause a woman to become pregnant just by looking at her.

My mother was a prude, so she would not have liked the stork theory so much if she'd looked into the etymology of the word *stork*. The stork was named for its thin, sticklike legs, the name coming from the German *storch*, which means *stick*. But it's also a slang word for penis.

Tawdry

The remarkable cathedral at Ely, just north of Cambridge in the U.K., stands on or near the site of a much smaller religious building that was established there in the 7th century by Etheldrida, a Queen of Northumbria. Sixty years after her death (in 697), the Venerable Bede recorded the nature of her passing, saying that she died of a neck tumor, a fate she ascribed to the wearing of necklaces in her youth. She eventually became the patron saint of Ely, but by the time that happened, the Normans had arrived on Albion's shores and Anglo-Saxon names like *Etheldrida* were as passé as punk rock, so she was referred to as St. Audrey.

Every 17 October, the populace honored her by holding a fair, where—along with toffee apples and goldfish-in-a-plastic-bag—they sold lace ribbons and scarves for wearing round the neck, presumably to commemorate the tumor.

Well, you know how it is with fairs like that: the apples aren't the best, the goldfish dies after a few days, and the lace falls to bits the second time you wash it. The term *St. Audrey's lace* was corrupted over time to *tawdry lace*, and all that's left now is the *tawdry* part.

Robot

It's not often that a Czech word makes it into the English language. Basically it's *polka, semtex,* and *robot*—that's about it. *Robot* comes from the 1920 play, *Rossum's Universal Robots,* by Czech author and science fiction writer, Karel Capek. The play is about a factory that makes artificial people called Robots, who are a bit like terminators in that they look human, they can think for themselves, and they eventually rebel against their human masters and try to wipe out the human race. What the original robots couldn't do was travel back in time or run for Governor of California. The term *robot* derives from the Czech word *robota*, meaning *work* or *compulsory labor*.

Hazard

The game of backgammon is very old. It's probably 5,000 years old or thereabouts. Certainly there are records of backgammon being played in ancient Mesopotamia and the game appears to be similar to the Egyptian game, *Senet*, which dates back to 3,000 BC. That puts a "latest date" on the invention of dice, since dice are required for backgammon, although it's possible that dice go back even farther in time.

Backgammon may be best known as a gambling game, but in the Arabic world it is also prized as a game that teaches children to count. The Arabs had simpler games for gambling with dice.

Indeed, the Arabic word for dice, *al zar*, is also the Arabic name for a gambling game which came into English under the name *Hazard* and became popular in taverns. The French gave the same game a different name: *Craps*, which is a corruption of *crabs*. The word *hazard* eventually took its place as a bona fide English word, even as the popularity of the game fell away. Both languages continue to employ the name of the game: the phrase *au hazard* to a French speaker means *haphazardly* to an English speaker. And vise versa.

Quintessential

You may remember the movie, *The Fifth Element*. I certainly do, but mostly because of the strangely beautiful Leeloo, the orange-haired female, played by Milla Jovovich, who dropped in on Bruce Willis.

According to the plot of this madcap movie—which I admit I had trouble following—and according to all manner of ancient metaphysicians (a couple of quasi-philosopher, monkish characters figure in the movie), the physical world is composed of four elements: earth, water, fire and air. Everything is made up of some combination of these four elements, even a Nintendo GameBoy with a flat battery.

So the ancient world is rocking along, perfectly happy with its four elements, until Aristotle pipes up and proffers the idea of a fifth element, which is not of the nature of the first four. According to Aristotle, this element permeates everything, has no qualities or substance, is immutable, and by its nature moves in circles. His fifth element is decidedly non-physical, spiritual even. That's where the word *quintessential* comes from, because *quintessence* is Aristotle's fifth element (from the Greek, via Latin, *quinta essentia*, fifth essence) which, as you might have noticed, is pretty hard to detect—so hard to detect that you will never get the opportunity to point any out to your kids.

Suffice it to say that Aristotle's theories once had more cred than they do now and, except as a plot point for movies, *quintessence* has changed with time and acquired a new meaning: *the very essence of.*

But, as Aristotle insisted, a characteristic of the fifth element is that it moves in circles. Well, we—it—have now come full circle. In the movie, it turns out that Leeloo is the personification of spiritual love—the thing that transcends the physical. She's the *quintessential* "Fifth Element."

X

COLLECTIVE NOUNS YOU DON'T KNOW

"Reality is nothing but a collective hunch." ~ Lily Tomlin

According to William Cobbett in *A Grammar of the English Language* (1818), collective nouns are nouns of number, or multitude, such as Mob, Parliament, Rabble, House of Commons, Regiment, Court of King's Bench, Den of Thieves, and the like. That's true enough, but those collective nouns aren't the fun ones.

I remember in some English lesson at some point in my education that we spent a whole half hour talking about collective nouns, the high point of the lesson being when our teacher insisted, much to our collective disbelief, that the collective noun for a gathering of crows was *a murder*. One of my classmates responded by asking whether the collective noun for English teachers was *a fabrication*.

Thinking of that amusing little interchange now, it seems to me that a *fabrication* is a more appropriate collective noun for a collection of collective nouns, since there appears to be neither rhyme nor reason in the selection of some of these words. It's as though a group of Oxford dons invented them all in an evening of heavy drinking. With that in mind, here is my fabrication of collective nouns that you are unlikely to know.

A Bale of Turtles

Excuse me, but when and where did anyone ever bale turtles? Cotton, hay and paper get baled, jute and sisal as well I shouldn't wonder, but turtles? Let me consult the dictionary. Okay, baling involves tightly wrapping and binding with rope, wire, cords or hoops.

If anyone baled turtles these days, the animal rights folks would be on it in minutes. So maybe that's it. Maybe the drunken dons came up with this in order to exasperate the animal rights people.

A Blessing of Unicorns

This wins the award for the most irrelevant collective noun ever, just nosing out the rarely used *necklace of hen's teeth*. Supposedly, it's really lucky to see a unicorn, so I guess seeing a multitude of them would simply scale up the amount of luck received. However, I'm not sure how anyone could know that, as I've searched high and low—exhaustively—and all the people who've seen unicorns are either in the care of men in white coats or choosing to stay anonymous. That makes it difficult to ascertain whether unicorns ever appear in a group. I presume they must, else how do they breed?

A Sloth of Bears

This is completely unfair. First of all you shouldn't be able to use one animal as the collective noun for another, at least not without there being a right of reply. If there's such a things as a *sloth of bears,* then it's only fair that there should also be a *bear of sloths*. But there isn't. There's only a *bed of sloths*. A *bed of sloths* works fine as a metaphor for these sleepy creatures, but actually, if the Goldilocks story is true, then a *bed of bears* would work fine, too.

It's possible that a *sloth of bears* is just a corruption of a *sleuth of bears*. This is an alternative but not much of one, because a sleuth is a very singular detective. Most likely, *sleuth* really comes from the Old English noun, which meant *animal track*. Bears certainly leave tracks and if *sloth* is a corruption of *sleuth*, then, when you follow a sleuth, you might find a sloth of bears. Of course, sloths climb trees and spend precious little time on the ground, so I guess it's unlikely we'd ever see a *sleuth of sloths*.

A Pulpititude of Preachers

This has to qualify as the worst of all collective nouns, in almost every respect. It could have been a lot better. It could have been a *humility* of preachers, or a *baptism* of preachers, or a *pontification* of preachers, or even a *hellfire* of preachers (if you like the rot-in-hell variety). It could have been a *blessing of preachers*, but the unicorns snaffled that one.

Come on. *Pulpititude* isn't even a real word; it's a clumsy, false construction that doesn't even pretend to be Greek or Latin. It's an abomination. Hey. That would have worked too, wouldn't it? An *abomination of preachers*?

A Pod of Whales

First let me tell you about a *pageant of iPhones*. (I'm making this up, of course, but perhaps I should propose it.)

About six months ago I went to the cinema to watch a movie and just about everyone in the audience over the age of three had an iPhone. I know, because when the request came up on the screen for the audience to turn off their cell phones, a pageant of iPhones appeared in the darkness and winked out one by one. The moment said, in no uncertain terms, "iPhone, therefore I am." How very sad.

Anyway, a *pageant* of iPhones is intuitively fine as a collective noun, whereas a *pod* of whales is completely counterintuitive. A pod is an elongated seed vessel, normally associated with leguminous plants. A *pod of whales* is thus one humongous pod. How does that make any sense? That's why you have schools, herds, and gams of whales—so you can avoid this ridiculous use of the word *pod*.

Thinking about it, how is the iPod pod-like anyway?

A Neverthriving of Jugglers

There is no collective noun for unicyclists, trapeze artists, lion tamers or tightrope walkers. So why is there a collective noun for jugglers? And why is the collective noun a *neverthriving*? I've surfed the web to find some reason to this and the only reference I can find suggests that the word was coined in the 15th century to indicate that juggling was a bad career choice. Naturally, economic circumstances change and *neverthriving* may not be the right word anymore, especially if you're a good enough juggler to work for Cirque Du Soleil.

A more modern collective noun might be a *doingquitewellactually* of jugglers, or in a recessionary climate, an *atleastigottajob* of jugglers.

A Sneak of Weasels

Some collective nouns seem just right and this is definitely the case with a *sneak of weasels*. It's not that weasels are particularly sneaky; it's just that they are characterized that way in A. A. Milne's book, *Toad of Toad Hall*. Weasels eat eggs, which might be thought of as a little sneaky, especially if you happen to be the mother bird.

As regards their own young, mother weasels carry them around in their mouths, rather than leave them in their burrows. You can call that sneaky if you want. As the babies grow, the families (or sneaks if you prefer) hunt together until the young finally move out. The *sneaks* that prey together stay together.

A Drudge of Skeletons

A drudge is someone who works hard at boring tasks; who works in a servile job and labors for scant reward. That's exactly the kind of work you get if you're a skeleton. First of all there's not much work, but you take what you can get. Most likely some medical college or other will hire you. You'll get to participate in anatomy classes and, admittedly, you'll be out there center stage. But it's the Professor of Medicine who gets to say, "The foot bone's connected to the leg bone; the leg bone's connected to the hip bone, etc." You just stand there looking fleshless. What can I tell you? *Atleastyougottajob*.

A Superfluity of Nuns

This sounds like it's intended to be a joke, but it may not be. Let me quote to you from the book, *Nuns and Nunneries: Sketches Compiled Entirely from Romish Authorities*, by Lewis Hippolytus Joseph Tonna (1852): "The second degree of poverty is to deprive yourself of whatever is superfluous; for the smallest superfluity will prevent a perfect union of the soul with God."

Nuns who have not yet achieved the perfection hinted at here, thus, both collectively and individually, represent a *superfluity*.

A Murmuration of Starlings

When I first ran into this collective noun I figured that it had to do with the *murder* of crows. In general, crows are carrion feeders and don't murder anything. They wait for some other species to do the murdering and they feed on the leftovers. Nevertheless, when it's murder out there, the crows will have a banquet. Ravens are equally enthusiastic about carrion, but the language is a little more circumspect in their case. So we speak of an *unkindness* of ravens.

My thought was that starlings probably just watch all this behavior, feeling mildly revolted, and murmur about it. But, no. To my surprise, I've discovered (oh, the power of the Internet) that starlings actually do murmur.

This collective noun is spot on. You can even watch and listen to the murmuring starlings on a video on the web at: http://bearcastle.com/blog/?p=1412.

XI

Units of Measure You Don't Know

"Nah, man, they got the metric system. They wouldn't know what the fuck a Quarter Pounder is." ~ John Travolta, playing the gangster Vincent Vega in Quentin Tarantino's movie, *Pulp Fiction*

I became interested units of measure when, quite a while ago, I read a book by Professor Alexander Thom, the man who discovered the megalithic yard. This bright Scottish professor suspected that the megalithic stone circles strewn across the British Isles and Northern France were probably arranged in some measured way. By surveying many of them he eventually deduced the unit of measure to be 2.72 feet, which he promptly named the *megalithic yard*. Sadly, it had been forgotten, discarded in the landfill of history when people ceased to care much where the sun rose on the solstices.

The megalithic yard was probably eclipsed by the much more popular cubit, which is also a bit passé. The cubit dates back to Ancient Egypt and the Pharaohs, who were inclined to build more impressive stuff. It is believed to represent the approximate length of someone's forearm, because the Egyptian hieroglyph for cubit shows a forearm. If so, then Ancient Egyptian forearms were 20.6 inches in length.

The Egyptian's were trendsetters in Ancient times, and pretty soon everyone had their own cubit: the Romans, the Greeks, the Jews, the Babylonians, and even the early Mesopotamians. Each such cubit was a different length. This must have made life difficult for international builders, shipwrights and cloth traders in ancient times, as in, "When I said I wanted my trireme 100 cubits long, I meant Egyptian cubits, you idiot!"

The origin of the modern yard is not known for sure, although it is suspiciously close to 2 cubits (not Egyptian cubits, you idiot, Roman cubits). The British Standard Yard was eventually defined as being the length of an official yardstick that was kept in the U.K.'s Houses of Parliament. It burnt up when the Houses of Parliament burnt down in 1834, so it was replaced by a more scientific measure derived from the swinging of a pendulum held in a temperature-compensated environment, in a vacuum, at sea level, in Greenwich—the place that's famous for its mean time.

The British yard was eventually usurped by the French *mètre*, with the Brits finally caving in and adopting the metre in 1964 (that's right: the spelling for U.S. English speakers is *meter*, but for everyone else in the world—in the internationally approved world—it's *metre*.)

Just as there is a story behind the yard, there is a story behind every unit of measure. Here are ten that you may not have heard:

Jigget

If you ever learned French, you'll know that the French can't count properly. They do okay on the small numbers and then they go completely weird once they get above sixty (*soixante*), and when they get to eighty (*quatre-vingt*), it's clear that they've lost it completely. There are two possible explanations for this:

The more obvious one has to do with the slyly suggestive number, *soixante-neuf* (69). When a Frenchman reaches sixty-nine, being French, he gets completely distracted and forgets what should logically come next. Instead of assigning a nice separate number for seventy, eighty, and ninety, he just starts adding tens or multiples of twenty—willy-nilly—to what's come before: *soixante-dix* (sixty-ten), *quatre-vingt* (four-twenty) and, the most egregious of all—*quatre-vingt-dix* (four-twenty-ten). *Sacre bleu!*

The theory that the French are just making this up is made more plausible by the fact that they are alone in this nonsense—even among other French speakers. Maybe it's just the Swiss being Swiss, but for French speakers in Switzerland, those numbers are as they should be: *septante*, *huitante* and *nonante*.

An alternative explanation for the irregularity, however, is that the French counting method, in France, is influenced by sheep counting.

Jigget is the number *20* in many sheep-counting systems and it means (wait for it…) *20 sheep*. Okay. Maybe you didn't know that such things as sheep-counting systems exist, but they do. And there are a surprising number of them. Seventeen different ones are known from different parts of England, including one each for most of the Yorkshire Dales. There are others throughout the Ancient Celtic region (Ireland, Wales, Scotland and Northern France), and there were even two discovered in the U.S., one in the Cincinnati area and another in Vermont.

The way the system works is that the shepherd herds his flock through a narrow gate at the end of the day, and counts the sheep one-by-one in groups of 20. He has a pocket full of pebbles and another empty pocket, and for every 20 sheep counted he shifts a pebble from one pocket to the other. If he comes from Swaledale in Yorkshire, these are the 20 numbers he uses:

Yan, Tan, Tether, Mether, Pip
Azer, Sezar, Akker, Conta, Dick
Yanadick, Tanadick, Tetheradick, Metheradick,
    Bumfit
Yanabum, Tanabum, Tetherabum, Metherabum,
    Jigget

It's just possible that the French proclivity for counting in 20s derives from sheep-counting. Indeed, it may have been frustration with this weird counting irregularity that encouraged the French to seek out sensible decimal systems for everything else: lengths, weights and currency. This eluded the British for the longest time with their inches, feet, yards, chains, furlongs and miles (units of length); ounces, pounds, cloves, stones, hundred-weights and tons (units of weight); and farthings, pennies, shillings, pounds and guineas (units of currency).

Yes. The very people who still suffer with the illogical *quatre-vingt-dix,* et al, went on to invent the *très logique* metric system. The French defined their supremely simple *mètre* as one ten-millionth of the distance from the equator to the North Pole through Paris. You might be thinking: "What's the difference between the measurement through Paris and that through any other city?" The answer is not much—but it's not nothing either, because the Earth is not a perfect sphere. So Paris is the reference point.

When it comes to units of measure, Paris is the world capital and the Brits have little to boast about except the fading glory of Greenwich Mean Time.

Tod

The talk of sheep seems bizarre in an age where counting sheep is an activity for insomniacs rather than shepherds. But it wasn't always so; sheep were once big business. In the time of Edward III (1312 - 1377), the export of wool from England accounted for three quarters of the country's revenue. Consequently, counting sheep was an important activity and the size of herds was registered. The census of sheep was a key economic indicator, a bit like the number of housing starts is in the U.S. today.

English wool was regarded as high quality in those days. Much of it was exported to the Hanseatic League of North German Cities, but as time passed more and more wool exports headed to Florence where the weavers and dyers turned it into high quality material for clothes and drapes.

To make the wool trade with Florence easier, Edward III adopted a new *aver-de-pois* system of weights based on the Florentine ounce of 437 grains, which had 16 ounces to the pound (lb.), rather than 15, which was the going rate in Britain before Edward made the switch. In the 15th century, the old hundredweight of 108 pounds (in what universe does 100 equal 108?) was adjusted upwards for cloff (natural wastage) to 112 pounds to become the modern British hundredweight. This divided nicely by 16 into sevens, giving us: 7 lbs. (the clove), 14 lbs. (the stone), 28 lbs., and 56 lbs. (the half-hundredweight). The 28 lbs. measure, when used for wool, was called a *tod*.

Slug

We're not talking mollusks here. A slug is a unit of gravitational mass; in fact it's a unit of mass equal to the mass that accelerates at 1 foot per second squared when acted upon by a force of 1 pound, which means that it has an apparent weight of 32.174 pounds. Unless you're studying high school physics or remember joyous hours spent doing that, you probably don't have a clue what that means. I could explain this better, I'm sure, but in the end the imperial system of measurements is just *so* 20th century! I'd prefer not to distract any bright young physicists who are reading this. They don't need to clutter up their brains with foot-pounds per square inch and other such irrelevant expressions of flaky metrication.

Suffice it to say that the now-redundant slug was once a proud unit in the gravitational foot-pound-second system, which held sway in the era when the sun never set on the British Empire and Brits like me laughed in the general direction of those Frenchies, with their *mètres* and *litres* and *dynes*.

Mutchkin

The Magna Carta proclaimed, "Let there be one measure and one weight throughout England." It might as well have added, "...and peace in the Middle East." It's almost as though the English like to mess with units of measure.

Take, for example, the sorry history of the pint. When the United States was founded, America behaved sensibly in adopting the British gallon as its basic unit of measure. It seemed sensible: a pint was a pound of water and a gallon was 8 pounds. It didn't take long for the British (in 1824) to upset the apple cart with a new imperial gallon deemed to be 10 pounds of water, upping the British pint to 20 fluid ounces.

Then, in the 20th century, the British got all European and went metric, dropping the pint except for the purposes of drinking beer. The Australians and New Zealanders followed suit as regards the beer, but upped the British pint from 568ml to 570ml. In Canada, the beer pint is 18 fluid ounces—the average of an American pint and a British pint—but no one is quite sure why.

The Scots disagreed with the English about drink and had their own beer pint, equal to a generous 3 English pints. A quarter of this measure was known as a *mutch-*

kin, but the word is anachronistic. Scottish pubs haven't served as much as a mutchkin for years.

Scruple

Pharmacists have scruples, or at least they used to, back in the day when they were called apothecaries and had their own guild. Apothecaries, believe it or not, once belonged to the Grocer's Guild, but, after flirting with the Guild of Physicians and Barber-Surgeons, they formed their own guild. This gave them a platform for arranging their own affairs. So, like many English men before them, they promptly defied the Magna Carta by inventing their own system of weights:

> 20 grains to the *scruple*
> 3 scruples to the *drachm*
> 8 drachms to the *ounce*
> 12 ounces to the *pound*

One can easily imagine the Guild meeting that was held to agree on this momentous slice of madness. Here's the transcript:

> *Chief Apothecary*: "I propose that there be 12 ounces to the pound, for did Our Lord not have 12 apostles?"
>
> *All*: "Hear, hear."
>
> *Chief Apothecary*: "And I propose that there be 8 drachms to the ounce, for be there not 8 notes in the octave?"
>
> *All*: "Yes, but what be a bloody drachm?"
>
> *Chief Apothecary*: "It be another word for dram, but it be sounding way more esoteric and special."
>
> *All*: "*Drachm* it be then."

> *Chief Apothecary*: "And let said drachm be further divided by three, expressing the triple nature of the Supreme Being."
>
> *All*: "Amen. How saintly and profound."
>
> *Chief Apothecary*: "And so that the people might know that we be men of good conscience, let us name the third part of the drachm the *scruple*."
>
> *All*: "How apposite! For we be mighty scrupulous fellows."
>
> *Chief Apothecary*: "And let us further divide the scruple into 20 grains, so that we may count the grains using one of the many sheep-counting methods that be current in our land."

And so it came to pass, until—thankfully—the system was ditched in the 20th century.

Dol

The passing mention of barber-surgeons above brings to mind the barbarous (or barberous) nature of dentistry. By and large, the surgeon part of the barber-surgeon's job was to bleed you with leeches or extract teeth without the inconvenience of anesthetic. That's why the traditional barber's pole is red and white—the white representing bandages and the red representing blood. Marketing at its most magnetic. You see a barber's pole and immediately think; "I must go in there and have a tooth pulled."

To my mind, dentists in the U.K. should be made to put barber's poles outside their surgeries. I remember once being suckered by a U.K. dentist. He chatted to me calmly about the psychology and perception of pain, and how some people have a very high level of tolerance to pain. He said that he had patients who simply preferred not to have injections of novocaine, as they could easily manage the pain of the drill. "What the hell," said I, "I'll try it"—thoroughly taken in by his sadistic subterfuge.

What can I tell you? It was emotional.

Anyway, the dol is the basic unit of pain. At Cornell University in the 1950s, James Hardy, Herbert Wolff and Helen Goodell carried out pioneering experiments on pain, asking subjects to report noticeable differences in the experience of pain caused by radiant heat directed at their foreheads and hands. One dol is the basic unit of experienced pain, equating to the faint sensation felt when heat rays are first applied to the skin. The scale goes from 1 to 10, with 10 dols being severe, intolerable pain.

Having a tooth filled without anesthetic equates to at least 12 dols on that scale and also rates very high on the scale of really stupid things I've done.

Chiliad

When we're not counting sheep, we count in tens: one, ten, hundred, and thousand. After that we break things into thousands: a million being a thousand thousands and a billion being a thousand millions, except in the U.K., where the billion is a million millions, but a billionaire is someone whose net worth is £1,000,000,000 (go figure).

Those groupings of one thousand are called *chiliads*. This isn't the only way of grouping numbers in order to count the big ones. The Greeks never bothered to count beyond 10,000—their word for 10,000 being *myriadis*, from which we get the word *myriad*, meaning *countless*. But at least they had a single word for ten thousand, which we don't have.

Surprisingly, the Chinese are more like the Greeks, but also more sophisticated. They group big numbers by *wan*, where a wan is 10,000. The Chinese (Mandarin) words for counting are: yi (1), shi (10), bai (100), qian (1000), wan (10,000). After that it's shi wan (100,000), bai wan (1,000,000), qian wan (10,000,000) and yi (100,000,000). The final *yi* here is pronounced differently to the *yi* that means *one*. (It only looks similar because of our inability to represent Chinese words and pronunciation adequately.)

The word *wan* is often translated into English incorrectly as 10,000, since the word also expresses the idea of *myriad*, meaning *a very large number*. Thus, the phrase, "may the Emperor live for 10,000 years" would best be translated as, "long live the Emperor."

The Chinese name for the Great Wall is *Wanli Changcheng*. It could be translated as the *10,000 li* wall (where a li is about a third of a mile), but it actually means *really, really long* wall.

Phon

I find subjective measures interesting. Ultimately, the dol is a subjective measure of pain. Similarly the phon is a subjective measure of loudness. Theoretically, the perception of loudness is related to both the pressure level of sound and its duration. The human auditory system works by averaging the effects of the sound pressure level over a window of between 60 and 1,000 milliseconds. This means that it can take you a whole second to realize how loud something is. The nervous system works like a computer as the sound persists, taking samples and averaging over this window, so if loudness increases or decreases you hear the difference.

Ultimately though, it's all subjective. You get used to a higher loudness and at some point you adjust; the nervous system accepts the new level as normal and filters accordingly. Advertisers on television know this, so they turn up the volume for the advert. Intelligent viewers know this too, so they buy TiVos and when they hear the noise level rise they know to fast forward past the insufferable adverts without even looking at the screen.

Centimorgan

A centimorgan is a map unit. As I'm sure you're aware, it is one hundredth of a morgan and approximately equal to a megabase. The *morgan* is eponymous, named for Thomas Hunt Morgan, who was a pioneer in the field of mapping.

What's all this about?

Not cartography, as I may have suckered you into believing, but genetics. There's a whole body of professionals working hard to improve our knowledge of genetics and of our health, as well. To them, the centimorgan is not an unfamiliar unit. In genetics, a centimorgan (cM) or map unit (mu) is a unit of recombinant frequency for measuring genetic linkage. To be precise: "The centimorgan is equal to a one percent chance that a marker at one genetic locus on a chromosome will be separated from a marker at a second locus due to crossing over in a single generation." I have no idea what that means; I just cheated and lifted the quote directly from the Wikipedia.

Darcy

I'm sure you read Jane Austin's novel, *Pride and Prejudice*, in high school, right? If, for some reason, your education never intersected with that book and you haven't compensated since by reading the graphic novel, watching the television series on PBS, or playing the video game, here's the story:

Elizabeth Bennet (Miss Prejudice) is one of five daughters who are stuck with a tough-luck-you're-female problem. Their father's property is entailed to a male heir upon his death, and there is no such heir. So they will be turned out of their house to fend for themselves unless they can find suitably wealthy husbands. Elizabeth runs into the haughty Fitzwilliam Darcy (Mister Pride.) They instantly dislike each other, he treating her as not-worth-a-dance-at-the-local-ho-down and she reacting with a who-the-flock-do-you-think-you-are. To cut a long story short, many things happen, then Mr. Pride falls in love with Miss Prejudice, but she rejects his proposal of marriage. Then some more things happen and Miss Prejudice falls in love with Mr. Pride and she accepts his second proposal. They get married.

If you read the novel and enjoyed it, you will no doubt see the sense in rating people's pride using Mr. Darcy as the standard and, hence, the *darcy* as the basic unit of measure. If we employ a decimal system—as Dudley Moore did to rate the beauty of Bo Derek in the movie, *"10"*—we arrive at a system in which the number 1 represents "not much of a darcy" and 10 equals "the full darcy."

However, the Brit in me argues for a more comprehensive measuring system. Indeed, we could and should default to the Swaledale sheep counting system. That gives us a 1-to-20 scale with a dick being a half-darcy, a bumfit being a three-quarter darcy, and a jigget being the full darcy.

Of course, I'm making this up. As much as it makes really good sense to be able to assess one's level of pride, there is no such system and no such unit of measure. The *darcy* is a geological measurement. It's a unit that measures the permeability of rock. Rock with a permeability of 1 *darcy* permits a flow of 1 cubic centimeter per second of a fluid with viscosity of 1 cP under a pressure gradient of 1 atmosphere per centimeter acting across an area of one centimeter. Unfortunately, although it sounds otherwise, the darcy is prosaic and mundane.

XII

IT Words You Don't Know

"We live in a society exquisitely dependent on science and technology, in which hardly anyone knows anything about science and technology." ~ Carl Sagan

In the lists of words that I've explored so far I've leaned quite heavily on archaic words that have fallen out of usage. Many such words refer to specialisms or specialist areas of activity that died out long ago. If we want to see how such words come into existence—eventually to fade from usage—then all we need to do is take a look at an area of specialism that is currently generating neologisms (new words) at a dramatic rate. Naturally I choose information technology (IT) and the Internet.

Here's a list of ten words that are almost certainly destined for obscurity…

Cancelmoose

I am a cancelmoose and I probably always will be—but only on a personal level. Ever since freemail services started up, I've managed several email accounts and now I have six, if you exclude a couple of derelict Yahoo mail accounts that I haven't used in years. I don't really care which of these email addresses anyone uses and I am resigned to the fact that at some point in time each email address will get onto a spammers list. Even if I don't provoke it by registering on some unscrupulous web site, it will happen, because someone with my address on his computer will get a virus that steals his email list and generously shares it.

However, I use Mac mail, which has a really good rules-definition capability and a good spam filter. As a result, most of the spam is dropped into a junk folder, where it lives for 7 days before it gets automatically deleted. I have set a rule that diverts all email from people in my address book to a special in-box and, thus, I get 3 kinds of mail: legitimate, questionable and junk. That's my cancelmoose strategy. A cancelmoose is someone who wages war against spam.

Teergrube

If you're a truly dedicated cancelmoose, then you'll want to set up a teergrube. *Teergrube* is a German word that literally means *tar pit*. However, the name is metaphorical, because a teergrube acts as a tar pit for spam and other malevolent email attachments such as worms. It doesn't stop all such traffic, but it does slow it down dramatically.

Teergrubes differ as to how they work, but they normally whitelist known good sources of email and blacklist known sources of spam, causing them to be delayed indefinitely or deleted. The rest can be analyzed before being let through.

Ohnosecond

An ohnosecond is a fraction of a second—in the region of one-tenth of a second. That's the time it takes for a person to realize that they've just goofed by doing something stupid or absentminded on a computer, such as forgetting to attach a document to an email or accidentally sending an email to an unintended recipient. The computer, being as dumb as a sack full of hammers, has no idea that you've just goofed and happily sends the email out without you having any means of intervention. Elizabeth Crowe coined the word *ohnosecond* in her book, *The Electronic Traveler*, and sadly it is almost certainly destined for extinction, because Google has now added an "Undo Send" feature to its heavily used Gmail service. Google holds every email back for 5 seconds and will cancel if you hit the "Undo Send" button. The ohnosecond, I fear, is no longer a fraction of a second.

Googleganger

Egosurfing is the term often used to describe the act of googling for your own name. If, like me, you have a really uncommon name (that's right, check the cover), then an egosurf will turn up references to you only. There will be no googlegangers in the mix. However, if I surf just on my surname, then the results are awash with googlegangers. A googleganger is someone who has the same name as you. Google, with its very limited grasp of semantics, is not smart enough to distinguish between the two of you, even if one of you happens to be guilty of numerous crimes against humanity. What could be worse than having a truly despicable googleganger?

Googleganger isn't the only word Google has given rise to; there is also a game called *GoogleWhacking*. This game challenges players to find a word combination that, when entered into Google, renders a single, solitary search result. Successful googlewhacks are difficult to pull off unless, like me, you run a blog site and therefore decide to put up a GoogleWhack page. I did this several years ago after I googled a combination of three words—*alien, sex, pills*—and discovered that Google gave me *no* results on that search. I promptly wrote a posting titled, "Alien Sex Pills." Et voilà: my first googlewhack.

Cyberchondria

This is another surfing term, referring to hypochondria caused by surfing to medical sites that give descriptions of the symptoms of given illnesses. If you're a doctor and one of your patients insists that he or she is suffering from pneumonic plague or blackwater fever, in all probability they are only suffering from cyberchondria.

Friendorphobia

A cyberchondriac might well suffer from friendorphobia, but not necessarily as a result of cyberchondria. I think most of us suffer from friendorphobia nowadays. Friendorphobia is the fear of forgetting a password. By the way, I'm serious—there is such a word.

Mobisode

When I first saw this word I simply couldn't work out what it meant. I guess I wasn't thinking in the right way. It is simply a compression of two words: mobile and episode. It refers to an episode of a broadcast television program that has been converted for viewing on a mobile device, such as an iPhone. The word was invented by the media industry rather than by geeks.

Advermation

I personally believe that the Internet will eventually include a much greater amount of *advermation* than it does now. And it will be a good thing. Internet advertising is often very intrusive and I would personally prefer to choose to read advertorial pieces than have flash animations dancing all over the screen. *Advermation* is, sadly, just another word for *advertorial* and, as such, doesn't deserve to exist as a word. Neither does *infotisement*, which also means *advertorial*. I have no idea why these two words have emerged when *advertorial* is not exactly an obscure word.

Crowdsourcing

There are a whole series of words that have been invented to describe relatively new approaches to employment. *Crowdsourcing* is one such word. It refers to the situation where a task normally assigned to a member of staff or a contractor is outsourced to a poorly defined crowd of people.

Open source developments are crowdsourcing of a kind. There are also mash up sites like ProgrammableWeb.com, where companies can host competitions in which the winner gets a prize for a program that carries out a specific function.

Other employment words worthy of note are: *permalancer* (a freelancer who hangs around forever), *homeshoring* (giving work to people who contract to work from home—thus cutting office costs), *cyberagents* (people who are willing to work on a homeshore basis), *presenteeism* (working extra hours and skipping holidays in order to try to preserve your job), and *decruitment* (what happens to you when your presenteeist efforts fail to impress).

Bozon

This is a nerd word; some people are accused of having a high bozon count. A bozon is the smallest possible quantity of stupidity that can exist independently of a body of stupidity. Some physicists take an atomic view of this, maintaining that a bozon is atom-sized and that if sufficient quantities of bozons accumulate in one place, critical mass will be achieved and something truly dumb will occur. However, other physicists argue that a bozon is a subatomic particle and if it collides at sufficient speed with other atoms that contain bozons, a bozon chain reaction will result and something truly dumb will occur. It doesn't matter which theory you adhere to; neither side of the argument has yet managed to inhibit the natural behavior of bozons.

The etymology of *bozon* is uncertain, but in all probability the *bozon* is eponymous; named from the fabricated individual Boso with whom Anselm of Canterbury (1033-1109) entered into debate in his writings. Anselm, a Benedictine monk and Archbishop of Canterbury, wrote treatises that consisted of dialogues between A (Anslem) and B (Boso). Boso just never seemed to get it right—clear evidence of a sorry accumulation of bozons. Indeed, it's doubtful that Boso ever really understood Anslem's famous ontological proof of the existence of God.

An alternative theory posits that the bozon is named for Alan W. Livingstone's Bozo the Clown, who was featured in read-along records released by Capitol Records in the U.S. in 1946 and thereafter. They sold in great numbers, leading to a pioneer TV show called "Bozo's Circus." This was a hit and Bozo had an extremely long and popular run on U.S. TV—his last appearance being in 2005. However, it is difficult to give much credence to this eponymy-come-lately bozon theory for three reasons:

- Bozo the Clown was not stupid; he was just a misunderstood entertainer.
- Nerds never watch TV unless it's science fiction.
- Nerds are deeply interested in ontological proofs of the existence of God.

It doesn't matter which theory you adhere to; neither side of the argument has yet managed to prove the etymological derivation of this relatively new word.

XIII

ADVENTUROUS WORDS

"Snakes. Why did it have to be snakes?" ~ Harrison Ford as
Indiana Jones, in the movie, *Indiana Jones and the Raiders
of the Lost Ark*

I've decided here to classify a word as adventurous if I
can make it relevant to my assembly of clichés from adventure movies. Call it artistic license or call it cheating, I
don't really care. By adventure movies I'm thinking of *Ro-
mancing the Tomb Raiders of the Lost Jewel of the Nile* and all
its many relatives, including nieces, nephews and distant
cousins. Such movies are about archaeological artifacts of
great value and the dangerous and daring deeds involved
in retrieving them.

Paleographist

If you want to retrieve an archaeological artifact, you
are going have to be a paleographist or at least pals with
one. Either will do, but it's probably best if you bring a
paleographist along, because then you'll have one handy
when you need to push the plot forward with his demise,
because nothing moves the plot along like a good murder.

Regardless, you (the hero of the tale) will have found
some fragment of papyrus or stone with ancient writing

on it and you'll need a paleographist to decode and translate it for you—better use him while you've got him.

A paleographist is an expert in the study of ancient writing and is expendable as soon as he has provided you with a clue on the whereabouts or meaning of the ancient artifact. The ancient artifact will, of course, be a halidom.

Viraginity

If you're going on a blockbuster adventure you will need a woman along—or if you're a woman you'll need a man along. Whatever. The point is, there needs to be at least one woman and one man in this movie and there needs to be a little bit of chemistry—and friction—between them, because Hollywood has demonstrated time and again that nothing of any value ever gets found on such adventures unless it is being sought by a loosely-coupled couple.

The woman, who will be pretty of course, will also need to be viraginous and as the plot advances, her viraginity will become increasingly evident. She absolutely mustn't lose her viraginity before the final scene of the movie because she's going to need it.

She'll find herself tied to a stake, or trapped in a cave, or forced to shinny up a rope to escape a writhing carpet of snakes. Whatever the peril and whatever the feat to be performed, she will be called on to demonstrate skills or qualities traditionally associated with a man—if only because the plot requires her to keep up with her heroic companion.

At the very least, she will need to be clever and brave, (and, for our entertainment, sarcastic), because at some point in the action, she will have to compensate for some wimpy, incapacitating phobia of his, and get them out of whatever jam they're in—like being tied together to a stake, entombed in a cave, or in the presence of something colubriform (shaped like a snake).

By now you've probably figured out that *viraginity* refers to the so-called "masculine" qualities of a woman, and that it is liberally used nowadays as a plot device, especially at the end of a movie.

Viraginity can make for an interesting twist on the typical "American Moment."

Poliadic (and Anthropomancy)

The heroic couple will surely get caught at some point by a tribe of natives who inhabit the location of the ancient artifact. They will not be pacifists. After they have caught our heroes, we will discover, to our horror, that the chief priest of the tribe is an anthropomantist. Our heroes can expect to be sacrificed in front of some poliadic idol, and their goose to be well and truly cooked. Fortunately, because of the inability of the natives to tie decent knots, or the presence of a shard of glass somewhere, or some other convenient plot device, our loosely-coupled couple will escape and they'll take the halidom with them. By the way, before I forget, *poliadic* means *relating to a local deity* and *anthopomancy* is *divination using human entrails*.

Halidom

If you are wondering why the natives turned out to be so hostile, doubtless it is because the ancient artifact our heroes have decided to retrieve is a halidom. That is also why, when the natives discover that our heroes have escaped, they will chase them in a furious manner, armed to the teeth with knives, spears, bows and arrows.

If you really want to rile a bunch of natives, steal their halidom. If they have several, steal them all. Technically, a halidom is any object considered holy or sacred. Ancient artifacts in adventure movies (arks, holy grails, crystal skulls, jewels of the Nile, etc.) are always halidoms. The next Indiana Jones movie will probably be called, *Indiana Jones and Another Goddam Halidom*.

Joola

So our heroes have escaped and they are trying to get away, chased by a band of natives with spears. They charge through the jungle and they come to the joola. The joola is the suspension bridge built out of ropes that crosses a chasm so deep that if you drop a stone into it you don't hear it hit the bottom until the end of the movie.

Our heroes start to cross the joola and, wouldn't you know it, the planks they step on start to break beneath their feet and tumble into the chasm, from whence no sound will come until the end of the movie. There can be only two explanations for this sudden failure of public infrastructure: either the joola maintenance team has been neglecting its duties or the joola itself is resistentialistic.

Resistentialism

I don't know about you, but I've experienced resistentialism and it's not pleasant. I don't support it and I'd be delighted if the stain that is resistentialism was banished from this planet and, indeed, the whole solar system.

I'm not going to embark on some philosophical diatribe that explains the logical contradictions within the whole resistential movement and condemns all its adherents. I'm simply going to say this: resistentialism is a plague on mankind. Enough.

If you're wondering what resistentialism is, it's the spiteful behavior of inanimate things. Adventure movies of this kind are rotten with resistentialism. Joolas are particularly prone to it, especially when they span deep chasms.

Schoenobatic (and Militaster)

Depending on how the joola fails, our heroes will either have to claw their way up out of the chasm on what remains of the joola after it comes apart—while the infuriated natives fire arrows and throw spears, of course—or they'll have to practice their schoenabatic skills while the infuriated natives fire arrows and throw spears. No matter which of these possibilities transpires, there's no possibility of our heroes getting wounded because the natives, infuriated though they may be, are all militasters.

Schoenobatic skills are skills of balance, particularly those relating to tightrope walking. What could be more welcome when you're practicing such skills under fire on a damaged joola that spans a deep chasm than to realize that all the natives are militasters—soldiers without any skills or ability—who couldn't hit a barn door with a blunderbus if they were sitting on the handle.

Hispid

By the time our male hero arrives at the joola, he will surely be hispid. The loosely-coupled couple have been captured and tied up for a while. Were it not for the fact that the militasters couldn't tie knots, they would probably never have escaped. They would no doubt be having their entrails read on some sacrificial slab by the high priest of the halidom.

In all the excitement—getting captured and escaping and whatnot—the hero will not have had time to shave and hence will be hispid, which means *stubbly or unshaven*. It's fashionable now for men—young men—to be hispid. But I suspect that our heroic woman's legs are pretty hispid by this time, too, although that's not something anybody wants to see on the big screen. I don't care how viraginous she is.

Humgruffin

Of course, the natives are only bit-part villains. The real humgruffin is the other archaeologist who wants to possess the halidom and hang it on the wall above his fireplace, where only he and his strangely unattractive mistress will be able to see it.

Our heroes are desperate to put the halidom in the care of the Smithsonian or the British Museum or some other place where artifacts hang out and have fun. Unfortunately, the humgruffin will appear with a gun when our heroes make it across the chasm and will take possession of the halidom leaving our heroes to fight off the militasters. Those militasters that have not tumbled into the chasm, from whence no sound will come until the end of the movie, will have made their way across a perfectly sound joola a few hundred yards down the track and will be pursuing our heroes again.

Humgruffin, by the way, simply means *a terrible person*.

Infracaninophile

You're probably an infracaninophile, like me, so when you get to the joola part of the movie you have no problem suspending your disbelief about the suspension bridge.

"Hey, rope frays and wood rots."

You're more concerned that our heroes escape from the vast horde of militasters that are chasing them, and that they overcome the shameful neglect of the joola maintenance team, and that they keep the halidom out of the hands of the humgruffin.

I often wonder when watching such movies whether there is anyone in the audience cheering for the militasters or the humgruffin. Probably not. The movie's director has convinced us, through various plot machinations, that our heroes face insuperable odds.

We all love the underdog—that's what an infracanin-ophile is, someone who supports the underdog—so we cheer for the loosely-coupled couple.

I don't need to tell you the rest, but I will. After risking their lives a few more times, the heroes will regain possession of the halidom and the humgruffin will meet a sticky end. The halidom will be put in the hands of a museum curator, who is the uncle of the female half of the loosely-coupled couple.

Finally, our loosely-coupled couple will have an American Moment to bring the movie to a close. As for the militasters, if they have any sense, they'll put more effort into practicing spear-throwing and archery and do their best to ensure that their joolas are better maintained in the future.

XIV

WORDS I PREDICT YOU
DON'T KNOW

"It's tough to make predictions, especially about the future."
~ Yogi Berra

Consider the following situation: A successful businessman, with a bundle of money, has a house in the Hamptons and a pied à terre in New York. He has a wife, several mistresses, a couple of kids and a drinking habit. One day his wife discovers the existence of the mistresses and storms off to consult her lawyers. His business tanks and he discovers that the fortune he's salted away in Bernard L. Madoff Investment Securities will return him less than a cent on the dollar. He has money hidden away in the Cayman Islands, but the IRS has got wind of it and they are making ambitious demands and writing threatening letter. In other words, he's reached a climacteric moment and his life sucks like a singularity.

What is going to happen? Perhaps all is not lost. Perhaps he'll come through this unscathed. He's definitely motivated to consult a fortuneteller to find out what the future holds.

As soon as this whimsical idea enters his brain he realizes that he has choices. He can go to a palmist or an astrologer or a Tarot reader or just a plain old card reader (a cartomancer). Maybe he prefers an I Ching specialist or a numerologist or a clairvoyant complete with crystal ball and gypsy costume. Or…

Maybe he wants something really exotic, like some form of divination he's never heard of before. You never know. He might discover someone who'll predict a really rosy future for nothing more than a fist full of dollars. But, what to choose? Here is a list of ten unlikely possibilities:

Stichomancy

Why not just grab the Yellow Pages, find the fortune-telling section, and choose the first name on the list? Not convinced that Fate works alphabetically? How about opening the Yellow Pages at random instead and putting your finger anywhere on the first page that presents it-self? If you do that, you'll be indulging in stichomancy—divination by randomly selecting a passage from a book. Don't ask me how you should interpret it if your finger alights on "Diamond Joe's All Star Strip-o-Grams," or "Larry's Low Budget Precision Plumbing." I know nothing of the technicalities of stichomancy.

But I can tell you that this form of divination has been popular in its time, because there are several words for it. In addition to *stichomancy*, it is also called *biblioman-cy*. If you confine yourself to using books of poetry, it's called *rhapsodomancy*. Remarkably, there are even terms for rhapsodomancy that date back to Roman times. They are: *Sortes Homerica*, divination using *The Iliad*, and *Sortes Virgilianae*, divination using *The Aeneid*.

By the Middle Ages everyone was using the Bible for this kind of stichomancy, but nowadays the Yellow Pages is probably as good as anything.

If you want to be thoroughly modern, you could try googlomancy—typing random words into Google and interpreting the meaning of the first web page link that comes up.

Logarithmancy

Suppose our soon-to-be-bankrupt businessman, who craves knowledge of the future, is a financial trader of some kind. If so, he might be interested in a form of divination that employs sophisticated mathematics. In that case, logarithmancy is for him. Technically, *logarithmancy* is defined as *divination using algorithms*, but actually it is just what it sounds like. The only form of logarithmancy on record used tables of logarithms. The use of logarithms in this way may have evolved from the fact that astrologers used tables of numbers to work out planetary positions, so a table of logarithms may have been an impressive prop for a fortuneteller to have on hand.

Possibly numerologists who were just no good at arithmetic used them. No one really knows, because the information about how logarithmancy worked (if it ever did) has been lost. It's likely that logarithmancy was used to predict the ups and down of the various markets that flourished as the merchant traders of the 17th century opened up the sea-lanes of the world. Logarithmancers may have made recommendations on when to buy and sell shares in the South Sea Company, and modern-day logarithmancers, if only they existed, would surely provide our nervous businessman with excellent advice on which derivatives to lose money on.

Gyromancy

Perhaps our once-successful businessman has studied management practices and is familiar with Management By Walking Around (MBWA). If so, what could be more appropriate for him than Metagnomy By Walking Around? Metagnomy, by the way, is another word for divination.

Believe it or not, there are two forms of MBWA (the metagnomy MBWA, not the management one): *ambulo-*

mancy and *gyromancy*. Ambulomancy involves watching someone walk from one place to another and gaining insight from observing the choices he or she makes en route. From this you deduce what kind of person they are and what their future is likely to hold. The second form of MBWA is much more fun. With gyromancy, the person whose fortune is being told spins around inside a circle drawn on the ground. Letters of the alphabet are placed around the perimeter of the circle. When the person falls over from dizziness, the gyromancer takes note of the letter he fell on or nearest to. He is then put back on his feet and continues this way—spinning and falling—until a message is spelt out. The neat thing about gyromancy is that it works just as well—maybe better—when used as a drinking game.

Coscinomancy

I am not making this up, but as I write this I feel as though I am. Coscinomancy is metagnomy using a sieve and shears. It was used long ago in Ancient Greece and as recently as the 17th century in Europe to determine the guilty party in a crime.

But that's the "why." Let's go back a minute to the "what"—to the *sieve and shears* part, because I know what you're thinking. You're thinking: *Huh?* Because that's exactly what I was thinking. You've got a coscinomancer standing there with a sieve and a pair of shears. What's his next move?

Seriously. How does that combination make any sense at all? Why is it not an iPod and a jar of pickles? Or a rubber bullet and a baseball bat? I wouldn't even mention this absurdity were there not an entire entry for coscinomancy in the Wikipedia.

Apparently, many writers throughout history have described coscinomancy, one of the most notable being a German magician. In 1533, Heinrich Cornelius Agrippa von Nettesheim wrote about this practice in his discourse, *Libri Tres de Occulta Philosophia*.

Well, I've read and read about this practice, about the sieve dangling from the shears and how a demon supposedly spins the sieve around to perform the alleged prognostication, and I *still* have no idea what coscinomancy is. Or, for that matter, what it does. I suspect that the only really good coscinomancers are dead coscinomancers, and that the only living practitioner of coscinomancy is the person who wrote the Wikipedia entry, and he (or she) isn't telling us the whole story.

Omoplatoscopy

Omoplatoscopy is much more believable than coscinomancy, although it is still a bit "out there." Omoplatoscopy is metagnomy using a shoulder blade (normally of an animal), which has been charred from being burned in a fire. The reason it's more believable is that there are so many words that relate to using a shoulder blade for metagnomy.

I have no idea why that particular bone has been selected for fortunetelling. There are no metagnomy methods I've come across that use any other bone. I guess it must be just the right shape for reflecting the future. Anyway, for the record, there's also *armomancy* and *spatulamancy*, which are words for metagnomy using an animal shoulder blade in general, and there's *scapulimancy*, which means precisely the same as *omoplatoscopy*.

Apantomancy

The previous two forms of metagnomy are unlikely to appeal to our challenged business leader, because (a) they are archaic, much like the regulation of Wall Street, and (b) practitioners are hard to come by, much like Wall Street regulators.

There are many forms of metagnomy, which you simply cannot do whenever you feel inclined. For example, practicing metagnomy that involves thunder (*brontomancy*) or lightning (*ceraunomancy*) means you're in a situation where "no thunderstorm equals no metagnomy."

Imagine how frustrating life must be for a haruspex—a fortuneteller who combines the observation of lightning with the examination of entrails—when there's no likelihood of a thunderstorm for weeks. You'd have to have some other form of metagnomy to resort to, certainly in a drought. In fact, if you were a haruspex, apantomancy would be the perfect alternative for when the thunder won't strut its stuff. Apantomancy is metagnomy using any object at hand—absolutely anything inanimate, no holds barred.

Related to this, I suspect, is the far more particular macromancy, which is metagnomy by studying the largest object in the area, and also the more exacting micromancy, which is metagnomy by studying the smallest object in the area. Both of these are excellent options that can be tried anywhere, with anyone, at any time. I suspect that once metagnomy brings itself more up-to-date with technology, we'll see the development of nanomancy, metagnomy using an electron microscope.

Taghairm

Maybe our sorry businessman has been on several of those intensive personal growth courses where everyone ends up meditating and hugging trees. In which case, taghairm really might appeal to him. It's a form of metagnomy in which the person seeking inspiration about the future is wrapped up snugly in the cozy, steaming hide of a freshly slain ox and deposited in the recess of a lonely waterfall or at the bottom of a precipice, there to lie for hours and hours, meditating on some weighty question or other about things to come.

This surreal art was practiced in the Scottish Highlands, but I don't see why it couldn't be equally effective wherever you do it. Okay, maybe not in Kansas, because of the lack of waterfalls and precipices—although, come to think of it, a really big highway fly-over might do the trick. And this is technically something you can do yourself, if you think you can pull it off, but you could also have a practitioner do it for you. In Scotland, they tended to choose a soothsayer, give him a weighty question, and then commence with the ox slaughtering. I'm confident our beleaguered businessman would feel fine about wearing a meat straightjacket.

Retromancy

You might think this means metagnomy using a method that was once popular and is now in revival. It doesn't; it is metagnomy by looking over one's shoulder. While metagnomy is usually about looking forward, retromancy is about looking forward while looking backwards. I'm not exactly sure whether there are any practicing retromancers nowadays, mainly because *retromancer* (a practitioner of retromancy) has recently acquired a new meaning: *a person or group or people dedicated to the revival of any and all things considered retro*—including retromancy, I'd hope. This makes it pretty much impossible to find yourself a retromancer on the Internet. Our sorry businessman might as well try kalling.

Kalling

Once again, I feel compelled to assure you that I am not making this up: Get a person, put a blindfold on him, then place a bunch of different varieties of cabbage in front of him. Still blindfolded, the subject picks up one of the cabbages and the particular type chosen reveals the future. That's right. Kalling is metagnomy based on the variety of cabbage a blindfolded person picks up.

Before you object to this, let's just review the facts here. There are over 400 different varieties of cabbage nowadays: round, conical, flat, curly, tight- or loose-leaved, green, white, red, and purple. There are only 64 hexagrams in the I Ching and that's been a popular means of divination since Wu was king of the Chou. So, depending on how many varieties of cabbage you can put your hands on, we could argue that kalling is every bit as subtle as the I Ching. Or not.

As with all of the other forms of divination we've been discussing, the challenge with kalling is not in performing the ceremony—or even an overabundance of cabbages. The problem is in finding someone who can tell you what the results mean. Where do you advertise for someone who reads cabbage?

Geloscopy

Geloscopy is metagnomy based on interpreting someone's laughter. For example, in early 2008, a noted geloscopist, on hearing Hillary Clinton's laugh, prophesied accurately that she would not become president. Geloscopy insists that people who laugh a lot are open and sincere; those who rarely laugh are persistent and reserved; quiet laughter says, "facile but kind"; loud laughter says, "harsh and inclined to lying"; and Hillary Clinton's laughter says, "vote for someone else."

The main challenge with geloscopy is getting the client to laugh, but practiced geloscopists have a sure fire way to pull this off. They simply tell the client about all the metagnomic absurdities described above and they're splitting their sides in no time.

XV

ENGLISH WORDS YOU DIDN'T KNOW WERE ARABIC WORDS

"She had perused the works of the poets and knew them by heart; she had studied philosophy and the sciences, arts and accomplishments; and she was pleasant and polite, wise and witty, well read and well bred." ~ A description of Scheherazade from Richard Burton's translation of *The Arabian Nights*

As the Roman Empire died, it came apart in the middle, splitting itself and the Christian Church between East and West. The border of the two halves ran between what is now Croatia and Bosnia Herzegovina. Roman Emperor Constantine was the unwitting architect of this division because he founded Constantinople as an alternative capital to Rome, in a place called Byzantium. The city was well positioned on trade routes and in a highly defensible situation. The Western half of the Roman Empire collapsed first, when the Huns took Rome. They did so in part by deliberately destroying the aqueducts, thus making it impossible for Rome to remain a city of a million people.

The Eastern half of the Roman Empire was gradually eaten up by the rise of Islam, although it was never completely overwhelmed until Sultan Mehmet II captured

Constantinople in 1453 and renamed it Istanbul (which, believe it or not, means *downtown*).

In the intervening period between the fall of Rome in the 6th century and the fall of Constantinople almost a thousand years later, the Arabic Islamic culture flowered. Its influence would probably have expanded much further were it not for two events.

The first was the very early schism in Islam between the Sunnis and the Shiites, which had the two sides fighting against each other rather than forging an empire. The second was the Mongol invasion from the East, which laid waste to all the Islamic cities along the Silk Road and smashed the Abbasid caliphate.

Nevertheless, traces of that once supreme Islamic culture can be found in our language in words that few of us would ever suspect derived from Arabic. Here are ten such words:

Check

The word *check* has multiple meanings, all of which come from the game of chess and the act, in that game, of threatening or *checking* the king. When you check the king you limit its movements. So the word *check* came also to mean *a ticket or token used to check against loss or theft*. So we have the checks (or *cheques* in the U.K.) that we write against our bank accounts. The Chancellor of the Exchequer, in the U.K., is the Minister of Finance, and the term *exchequer* derives from the Anglo-French word *escheker*, which was a cloth divided into squares in the manner of a chessboard, which was used for reckoning revenue amounts.

All of this comes from the Medieval Latin *scaccus*, which in turn comes from the Arabic *shah* (ultimately Persian in origin), meaning *king*. The word chess comes from the French *échecs*, which has the same origin, as does the game of checkers, in which the word *check* is never used.

Admiral

There are lots of Arabic words for *leader* indicating kinds and ranks. *Caliph* literally means *successor*, referring specifically to the successor to Mohammed, and hence implies both a civil and religious leader who is a representative of Allah on earth. It is a little like the European idea of a King that rules by divine right. *Sultan* simply means *sovereign*. A vizier is nothing more than a high official in a Muslim government (the word means *public servant*) and a pasha is similar but in a military position. A sheikh is normally the leader of a tribe (or family). The word literally means *old man*. *Imam* generally refers to a religious leader, but specifically means the *leader of a mosque*. A mullah is also the leader of a mosque, but the word has the connotation of *master* or *learned*. An emir (*amir* in Arabic) is a ruler or commander. The *amir-ar-rahl* is the chief of transport, which on the seas means *head of the navy*, and that's where the word *admiral* comes from.

Magazine

The use of the word *magazine*, referring to a periodic publication, comes from the word *magazine*, meaning *military store*. For obvious reasons, military stores used to keep lists of what they contained and printed them on a regular basis. That's how the word for the published magazine evolved, conceived probably to mean *storehouse of information*.

It's also where the word for a magazine, meaning *a container holding cartridges or bullets*, came from. However, the use of the original word *magazine* as a military store faded away. We are now more likely to refer to a military store as an arsenal, although arsenal originally had the meaning of *the place where the weapons were manufactured*.

Both these words, magazine and arsenal, come from Arabic. Magazine comes from the Arabic *makhazin*, which means *storehouse*, and arsenal comes from *dar as-sina'ah*, which means *factory*. In Arabic, neither word specifically implies the making or storing of weapons.

Saracen

You probably suspected that the word Saracen had Arabic origins, but you probably didn't know that it literally means *easterners*. The word is found in Roman and Greek (*saracenus* and *sarakenos*) and was used to describe the nomads of the Syrian and Arabian deserts. The word entered our language from the Arabic *sharquiyin* from *sharqiy*, which means *eastern or towards the sunrise*.

There are other words we commonly hear that have quite specific Arabic meanings that you're probably unaware of: *Islam* comes from the word for *submission*, *Sunni* simply means *lawful*, and *Shiite* comes from *shiya*, meaning *sect*. *Koran* literally means *recitation*, whereas our *bible* comes from *biblion*, the Greek for *paper or scroll*. *Taliban*, which you might think refers to something fearsome, comes from the Arabic *talib*, meaning *student*.

Monsoon

If you want to understand Arabic culture, it helps if you understand a little bit about Islam. Muslims are expected to go on a *hadj* (a pilgrimage to Mecca) at least once in their life, if their circumstances permit. There is a pilgrimage season, which begins at the end of Ramadan, the month of fasting and the ninth month in the Islamic calendar. It lasts for about 60 days ending in a feast. A person who has been on a pilgrimage to Mecca is referred to respectfully as *hadji*.

The pilgrimage season is important because, if you go on a hadj to Mecca at any other time of the year, it counts as only half a hadj. Similarly there are other Islamic places of pilgrimage, which count as only half a hadj, no matter what time of year you turn up. Only Mecca counts as a full hadj. Mecca is where, according to tradition, Allah revealed the Koran to Mohammed.

So what does any of that have to do with a monsoon? The Arabic word *mawsim* refers to the appropriate season for a voyage or pilgrimage. This worked its way into Portuguese as the word *monção*, which was later used to describe the seasonal winds blowing in the Indian Ocean. This eventually became the English word *monsoon*.

Betelgeuse

Arabic astronomy was quite advanced and has left its traces accordingly. The Arabic calendar is lunar, so there was a need to keep an eye on the moon, calculating times for each new moon, the lengths of the solar year, the sidereal year, and whatever else is necessary to make a lunar calendar behave itself.

Arab astronomers posited the idea of a heliocentric solar system well ahead of Copernicus, observed the largest supernova in recorded history (about one quarter as bright as the moon), and even discovered that the earth had an elliptical orbit. One Abd al-Rahman al-Sufi, who specialized in recording a map of the stars, described the Andromeda Galaxy as "A Little Cloud" centuries before German philosopher, Immanuel Kant, proposed the idea of a galaxy. It should not surprise us then that so many of the stars have Arabic names.

Betelgeuse comes from *yad al jauza*, which means *hand of the jauza*, *jauza* being the Arabic name for the constellation Gemini, and for Orion as well. Medieval scholars later mistranslated the letter *y* as *b*, leading to the Medieval form, *Bedalgeuze*. The name *Rigel*, the bright star at the foot of Orion, comes from the Arabic word *rijl*, meaning *foot*.

Elixir

You are probably aware that English words beginning with the prefix *al* are likely to be Arabic in origin, since the Arabic definite article is *al* (in English, *the*). So it shouldn't be too surprising that all the following words come from Arabic: alcove, alembic, alfalfa, algebra, algorithm, alkali, almanac, alchemy and alcohol. *Alcohol* is a little odd because the Arabic *al-kuhul* refers to a fine metallic powder used as a cosmetic to darken the eyelids. When it moved into English, the definition expanded to mean *the distilled or pure spirit of something*, from whence came its modern meaning of *the intoxicating ingredient in beer, wines and spirits*.

Elixir ought also to be one of these *al* words, because it comes from *al-iksir*, which, it is believed, originally referred to a powder for drying wounds. Ultimately it came to mean a *liquid*, and particularly a liquid that the alchemists believed would confer immortality and that they could create from the "philosopher's stone." Arabic alchemy predates alchemy in Europe.

Sahara

Himalaya means *abode of snow*, so the Himalayas are the abode-of-snow-mountains. *Andes* comes from Quechua *andi*, meaning *high crest*, so the Andes are the high-crest-mountains. *Sierra* means a *range of mountains*, so the Sierra Mountains are the mountains-mountains. This redundancy in words is called a *pleonasm*. Both Gobi Desert and Sahara Desert are pleonasms. *Gobi* is Mongolian for *desert* and *Sahara* comes from *cahara*, Arabic for *desert*. They are desert-deserts.

Coffee

There's an awful lot of coffee in Brazil, but there didn't use to be. Coffee plantations weren't established in Brazil until 1727. England was already mad for coffee in the 17th century; in 1675, over 3,000 coffee houses were plying their trade there. Coffee had appeared in Europe, coming from Arabia, over a century earlier.

Yemen was the first great coffee exporter and it was such a lucrative trade that the government banned the export of any coffee plants for any purpose. Nevertheless, a Muslim pilgrim managed to smuggle some coffee beans out and raised coffee crops in India, and it spread from there.

The Arabic word for coffee is *qahwah*, which probably derives from the Kaffa region of Ethiopia, which is the original home of the plant.

Garble

There are a host of Arabic derived words I've not been able to cover, including: adobe, apricot, candy, cork, cotton, gazelle, ghoul, giraffe, jar, lime, mask, mattress, mohair, orange, safari, sofa, spinach, syrup and zero. Every one of these words has Arabic roots but I've limited myself to ten, so none of them makes the list.

My final word is *garble*, which distinguishes itself from the rest of the list by having lost its original Arabic meaning. Today's English word *garble* means to *corrupt, falsify, distort* or *scramble*.

In shipping, garbling is the practice of mixing rubbish with genuine cargo. However, the original Arabic word *gharbala* means *to sift*—sifting being a process used in refining and selecting spices.

The meaning has been lost in translation over time, the original meaning being thoroughly garbled.

XVI

WORDS WITH LIMERICKS

"… the limerick is the unrefiner's fire. It is as false and lifeless, as anonymous, as a rubber snake, a Dixie cup. It is indeed the dildo of desire! No one ever found a thought in one. No one ever found a helpful hint concerning life, a consoling sense. The feelings it harbors are the cold, the bitter dry ones: scorn, contempt, disdain, disgust. Yes. Yet for that reason, nothing is more civilized than this simple form." ~ William H. Gass in *The Tunnel* (1995)

This is completely vicarious. Nothing ties together this list of words except for the fact that each definition is accompanied by at least one limerick, some of them borrowed from elsewhere. Here are ten obscure words with limericks:

Longiloquence

I'm a strong believer in the idea that more people would use dictionaries if all the definitions were written as limericks. (There is no word for this belief, possibly because it's not a common belief.)

Nevertheless, if dictionaries were written that way, people would certainly remember the words a lot better. However, there are a few problems with the idea. Writing definitions is a lot easier than writing limericks. Some words just don't scan well, especially multisyllabic ones.

A good number of the definitions would surely suffer from longiloquence. Apropos of which:

> In a limerick let me condense
> The meaning of *longiloquence;*
> It's about using herds
> Of nouns, pronouns and verbs
> When just one word or two would make sense.

Longiloquence means *using far too many words*. This is something that distinguished, for example, the poet who came from Raton from the poet who came from Peru, as demonstrated by the following two limericks:

> A poet who came from Raton
> Wrote a poem that went on and on
> For ages and ages
> 'Cross pages and pages
> Completing on page 91

Whereas…

> There once was a man from Peru
> Whose limericks stopped at line two.

(Origin: http://www.alphadictionary.com/fun/limericks.html)

Immaterialism

It's not impossible to work out the meaning of this word and anyone steeped in philosophy will probably know it. Despite the fact that it sounds like a doctrine based on the observation, "Pardon me, but you've clearly mistaken me for someone who gives a damn," or more famously, "Quite frankly, Scarlet, I don't give a damn," it is not.

Immaterialism is the theory that material substance does not exist at all and that the universe is created entirely by minds and the ideas that inhabit them. This idea was propounded by Bishop Berkeley in the 18th century and summarized in his motto *"esse est percipi"* (to be is to be perceived).

To lampoon this philosophical speculation, Monsignor Ronald Knox wrote the following limerick:

> There once was a man who said, "God
> Must think it exceedingly odd
> If he finds that this tree
> Continues to be
> When there's no one about in the quad."

Amphigory

A question that may have sprung to your mind when reading that limerick is "Was that an amphigory?"

Of course, that's only possible if you know what *amphigory* means. An amphigory is a poem that seems profound, but is really complete nonsense. I'll provide an opinion of Knox's limerick later, but the following is definitely an amphigory—or is it?

> There once was a man who said, "Though
> It seems that I know that I know,
> What I'd like to see
> Is the I that knows me
> When I know that I know that I know."

(Origin: *The Way of Zen* by Alan W. Watts)

Ergophobia

Having already struck a philosophical note with immaterialism, you may be guessing that ergophobia is related to the same subject, via Descartes. As in:

> The words *cogito ergo sum*
> Were met with opprobrium

When they came from Descartes,
Who was normally smart,
But in Latin, fallaciously dumb.

Ergophobia should, in my humble opinion, refer to the morbid fear of the Cartesian fallacy—*cogito ergo sum*—although, I suppose that word would be better conceived as *cogitoergophobia*. Sadly, there is no such phobia. It exists only here on this page and will probably never travel any further. Ergophobia is more prosaic. It means *the fear of hard work*.

Qualtagh

It's really unlikely that you'll deduce the meaning of *qualtagh* from the following limerick, but there's an outside chance, so let's give it a shot.

When you venture out onto the street,
Your friends and your neighbors to greet,
Having left your abode,
And stepped onto the road,
A qualtagh's the first one you meet.

It isn't that the limerick doesn't explain *qualtagh*, it's just hard to fathom there being a word which means, precisely, *the first person you run into after leaving your house*.

Qualtagh is Manx in origin and it literally means *first foot*. In the Isle of Man, which is steeped in Celtic heritage, there's a superstition about the person you meet after leaving your house. According to the superstition, it's considered fortunate if the qualtagh is someone whose complexion is dark, and unfortunate if they are a blonde or a redhead.

This superstition links with superstitions that surround the New Year in the U.K. and particularly in Scotland, where the first person to set foot in your house after the turning of the year is considered a good or bad omen, according to his or her height and hair color. This person can also be thought of as a qualtagh, being the first foot crossing the threshold. Coming or going... Either way, the superstition seems to apply.

Selcouth

There can be little doubt that the word *selcouth* is connected, in origin, with the word uncouth, but what could the prefix *sel* actually mean? Here's a limericky clue:

> A lush once proclaimed, "It's the truth
> That Kir Royale is selcouth,
> And so's Demanovka
> When mixed with peach vodka,
> And Grenadine mixed with vermouth.

If you've not tried any of these cocktails, you will not know how strange, unfamiliar and marvelous they are, but they are, and that's what *selcouth* means: *strange, unfamiliar, marvelous*. In particular, it refers to a combination of strangeness with wonder. Indeed, the word *selcouth* may itself be selcouth.

Misocainea

This is one of those words for a mania that doesn't end with the suffix *mania*, and that makes it an excellent candidate for a limerick:

> There was an old man from Lithuania
> Who once heard the word *misocainea*.
> He hated that word;
> T'was a word he'd not heard;
> Misocainea was plainly his mania.

Misocainea is the obsessive hatred of anything new or strange, such as, in the case of the old Lithuanian, any word he didn't know.

Philalethe

You can get a sense of the meaning of this word if you know that, in Greek mythology, the Lethe (pronounced LEE-thee) was one of the several rivers of Hades, the underworld. I seem to remember that something happened to those who drank the waters of the Lethe, but I'm damned if I can recall what it was.

> A philalethe is a what?
> I'd define the word in a shot,
> If I knew what it meant,
> But despite my intent,
> I'm afraid that I went and forgot.

A philalethe isn't just someone who forgets things; it's someone who does so with great enthusiasm. It's someone who loves forgetting.

Pancosmism

This word may well be known to those studying philosophy but unlikely to be used outside that field. We can define *pancosmism* with the following words:

> We can define a Pancosmist
> As someone who's going to insist
> That all things ethereal
> Are either material
> Or else they don't really exist.

Thus pancosmism is fundamentally atheistic since it denies the duality of God and universe, insisting that only the universe exists.

You're wondering how this differs from materialism? Materialism is more constrictive. Materialism is a child of pancosmism, but it provides a central emphasis on matter, insisting that only matter exists and that all phenomena are a manifestation of matter. Materialism is directly opposed by vitalism, which insists that all phenomena are, in some way, a manifestation of life. Vitalism is also pancosmic and atheistic.

Immanence

Immanence is definitely not *imminence*, which means *liable to happen soon*. In fact, *immanence* circles us back to the second word in this list and the limerick it rode in on. If you've seen that limerick before, then you'll probably know that it is one of a pair. Here they are together:

> There once was a man who said, "God
> Must think it exceedingly odd
> If he finds that this tree
> Continues to be
> When there's no one about in the quad."

> Dear Sir, Your astonishment's odd.
> I am always about in the quad,
> And that's why the tree
> Will continue to be,
> Since observed by
> Yours faithfully,
> God.

The good Mr. Knox is simply pointing out the immanence or omnipresence of God. Immanence might be thought of as synonymous with the word *omnipresence*, but the meaning is slightly different. An omnipresent God will doubtless be "always about in the quad," whereas an immanent God is not merely present in the quad, but actually inhabits or pervades the fabric of the quad.

Either way, these two limericks are not amphigories; they are reasonable objections to the philosophical ideas proposed by Bishop Berkeley.

XVII

Nonsense Words You Don't Know

"A little nonsense, now and then, is relished by the wisest men." ~ Willy Wonka in Roald Dahl's book, *Charlie and the Chocolate Factory*

In my humble opinion, nonsense should be relished by everyone. There's something magical about it. But I'm horribly biased, because my mother fed me nonsense from an early age. She had a perfect memory of a vast array of it, including everything from Liverpool street songs to Edward Lear. This list of ten words, which relate in one way or another to nonsense, is dedicated to her.

Verbigerate

To *verbigerate* is to *repeat nonsense or clichés* or just about anything meaningless. Young children verbigerate all the time. As far as I'm concerned, when my mother taught me doggerel of one form or another, she was simply filling the space that gets filled nowadays with TV adverts and pop songs. She taught me utter rubbish, like:

> Supposing supposing,
> The park gates were closing,
> And you'd got your nose in,
> Supposing, supposing.

And she would smile every time my brother or sister or I came out with that—which was far too frequent for most people's tastes. She also taught me some truly distilled silliness with not a word of sense in it. For example:

> Rah rah racker rah
> Racker rah rooney
> Ecka pecka
> Curiecker
> Rum tum tush

I have no idea what that is or where it came from or if it was ever intended to mean anything. I've surfed for it on the web. It's not out there as far as I can tell. It's nonsense handed down like an heirloom, and, for some reason, I'm grateful for it. My mother dealt only in whimsical nonsense, and in that field she was formidable. She was no blatherskite.

Blatherskite

A blatherskite is a garrulous talker of nonsense. The word is normally used in a pejorative manner to describe fishwives discussing the vicar's legs and the price of eggs. For me it brings up an image of the Gabblerdictum, a creation of an early British television puppet show called "Space Patrol." The Gabblerdictum was a Martian parrot taught to speak by the Irish genius, Professor Haggarty— but it didn't really speak, it just gabbled. The Gabblerdictum was an amusing character and its utterances were charming in the way that nonsense can be charming.

Idiolalia

Idiolalia is the use of a language invented by the person using it. The invention of a whole language happens very rarely, but the invention of entirely new words is not so uncommon. Nonsense poets, notably Lewis Carroll and Edward Lear, have invented many completely new words. Carroll's poem, "The Jabberwocky," is riddled with them. Edward Lear was less prolific, but still brilliant. His major idiolalic contribution to the world is the word *runcible*. What does it mean? Actually, no one has a clue. In "The Owl and the Pussycat," Lear writes:

> They dined on mince and slices of quince,
> Which they ate with a runcible spoon.

And in "Twenty-Six Nonsense Rhymes and Pictures," Lear's entry for the letter *D* reads:

> The Dolomphious Duck,
> Who caught Spotted Frogs for her dinner
> With a Runcible Spoon.

In Lear's illustration for the entry, he fashions the allegedly *runcible* utensil as a long-stemmed spoon with a large ladle-like bowl at the end, which possibly explains why my father always insisted that *runcible* meant *big*.

Illustration by Edward Lear

However, in another Lear poem, "The Pobble Who Has No Toes," he writes of the Pobble:

> He has gone to fish for his Aunt Jobiska's
> Runcible Cat with crimson whiskers!

There's no indication that Aunt Jobiska's cat was inordinately large. Lear also refers in other writings to a runcible hat, a runcible goose, and a runcible wall. If you can think of a quality shared by a spoon, cat, hat, goose and wall, then maybe you can come up with a credible meaning for this word. If you do, please let me know.

Remplissage

Literally, *remplissage* means *padding*, but it frequently refers to the use of padding in literary or musical works. For example, there are many pop songs that include nonsense remplissage, because the composers simply couldn't think of words to fit or fill out a lyric.

So, from the Beatles we get: "Ob-la-di, ob-la-da, life goes on, brah!… Lala how the life goes on…" They never replaced the nonsensical placeholder phrases—the remplissage—they used as they wrote the song, having concluded, presumably, that it worked fine as it was.

The Beatles also gave us, "Na na na na na na na na, na na na na, hey Jude…." But it's not just the Beatles who enjoyed a little nonsense padding now and then. Rock and roll, in general, is fertile ground for remplissage.

For non-Beatle examples, try Steam's, "Na na na na, na na na na, hey hey hey, goodbye." Or Gene Vincent's, "Be Bop A Lula, she's my baby. Be Bop A Lula, I don't mean maybe."

I strongly advise readers who remember the group, Middle of the Road, not to think about "Chirpy Chirpy Cheep Cheep." And I just as strongly advise those of you who do not know this peppy little piece of bubblegum, *not* to go look up the clip of it on YouTube. Do *not* let this song into your head!

Too late? Ah well, you can't say I didn't warn you.

Berceuse

Berceau is French for *cradle*, and a *berceuse* is a *lullaby*. It's not much of a stretch to see why lullabies belong in this section of the book, is it? They are invariably nonsense songs and the reason is obvious. Anyone who has ever gotten up (repeatedly) in the night to try to soothe a crying baby knows that any song you sing at that hour isn't going to make much sense. You are so tired and so sleep-deprived that you'd be hard pressed even to remember the words to this old standby:

> Hush, little baby, don't say a word, Papa's gonna
>   buy you a mockingbird
> And if that mockingbird won't sing, Papa's gonna
>   buy you a diamond ring
> And if that diamond ring turns brass, Papa's gonna
>   buy you a looking glass
> And if that looking glass gets broke, Papa's gonna
>   buy you a billy goat
> And if that billy goat won't pull, Papa's gonna buy
>   you a cart and bull
> And if that cart and bull turn over, Papa's gonna
>   buy you a dog named Rover
> And if that dog named Rover won't bark, Papa's
>   gonna buy you a horse and cart
> And if that horse and cart fall down, you'll still be
>   the sweetest little baby in town...

Complete and beautiful nonsense.

Brimborion

A brimborion is something that is useless or nonsensical. Hence, the "Mockingbird" song—the berceuse I just provided the lyrics for—could be described as a brimborion were it not for the fact that it has put kids to sleep for years. It certainly isn't useless, but some nonsense certainly is.

There's a range of opinion on this. The philosopher George Santayana said that nonsense was "so good only because common sense was so limited." Frederick Saunders maintained that "Nonsense is to sense as shade to light; it heightens effect." Agatha Christie insisted that nonsense is "completely unimportant. That is why it is so interesting!" E. M. Forster chimed in with "Nonsense and beauty have close connections."

But Douglas Adams pretty much hit the nail on the head when he wrote in *The Hitchhiker's Guide to the Galaxy*: "Totally mad. Utter nonsense. But we'll do it because it's brilliant nonsense."

The truth of the matter is that nonsense can indeed be brilliant and any nonsense that is brilliant is not truly brimborionic.

Macaronics

Nonsense can also be sophisticated. Macaronics, for example, is sophisticated nonsense verse. The term derives from the Italian *maccaroni* and was given to the world by Teofilo Folengo who, in his discourse, *Liber Macaronices*, described his verses as a literary analogue of maccaroni. He then defines *maccaroni* as a rustic mixture of flour, cheese and butter. Macaronics involve mixing Latin words with other words from normal language, producing semi-profound nonsense. An American, J. A. Morgan, wrote the best-known macaronic poem. You'll appreciate it if you have a smattering of Latin, otherwise you'll think it's a brimborion. It reads:

> Prope ripam fluvii solus
> A senex silently sat;
> Super capitum ecce his wig,
> Et wig super, ecce his hat.
>
> Blew Zephyrus alte, acerbus
> Dum elderly gentleman sat;
> Et capite took up quite torve
> Et in rivum projecit his hat.

Contra bonos mores, don't swear,
It is wicked, you know (verbum sat),
Si this tale habet no other moral
Mehercle! You're gratus to that!

Galimatias

There are many words that mean *nonsense*. For example: rubbish, gibberish, claptrap, balderdash, blarney, hogwash, baloney, rot, moonshine, garbage, jive, tripe, drivel, bilge, bull, guff, bunk, bosh, eyewash, piffle, mumbo jumbo, phooey, hooey, malarkey, hokum, twaddle, gobbledygook, codswallop, flapdoodle, bunkum, tommyrot, fatuity, poppycock, and prattle.

We probably don't need another one, but *galimatias* (alternate spelling, *gallimatias)* predates most of those listed above, and it's slightly different in the sense that the word indicates that something is meaningless rather than absolutely nonsensical. It is, perhaps, the most polite word that indicates nonsense. The etymology is uncertain but it probably derives from the French. In 16th century France, the Latin word *gallus* (literally *cock*) was student slang for a candidate engaged in a doctrinal dispute. The Greek *mathia* refers to learning. The derivation seems to imply that *galimatias* is specifically *academic* nonsense, the kind of poppycock spouted by a *gallus.*

Cromulent

This is yet anther word for nonsense, but it's thoroughly modern, having been invented by David Samuel Cohen (a.k.a. David X. Cohen), an American television writer, head writer and executive producer of "Futurama," and scriptwriter for "The Simpsons." It first occurs in an exchange between two schoolteachers in a "Simpsons" episode, "Lisa the Iconoclast":

Edna Krabappel: Embiggens? I never heard that word before I moved to Springfield.

Miss Hoover: I don't know why. It's a perfectly cromulent word.

Both *embiggen* and *cromulent* are newly coined words, but *cromulent* has passed into the language. It has a very specific meaning and use; it means *legitimate* and it can be used only ironically. Therefore, *cromulent* implies a complete lack of legitimacy. *Cromulent* is therefore one of those rarest of words in that it is self-referential. The word *cromulent* is undoubtedly cromulent.

Pasquinade

A pasquinade is a parody, either in verse or prose, and often anonymous. The term comes from the Latin word *Pasquin*, which was an old and damaged, dug-up-from-long-ago statue in Rome, erected at the corner of Piazza di Pasquino at the beginning of the 16th century. On Saint Mark's Day (April 25th), the marble torso of the Pasquin was dressed in a toga, and anonymous epigrams in Latin were attached to it, usually criticizing local notables from the government or the church. As the age of printing had arrived, these *pasquinades* were collected and published annually. So the original pasquinade was an acerbic epigram, but the word has come to mean *a parody of any kind*.

A poem that has probably given birth to more pasquinades than any other is Henry Wadsworth Longfellow's "Song of Hiawatha." The poem's galloping meter is probably responsible for this:

By the shores of Gitchee Gumee
By the shining Big-Sea-Water
Stood the wigwam of Nokomis,
Daughter of the Moon, Nokomis.

Dark behind it rose the forest,
Rose the black and gloomy pine-trees,
Rose the firs with cones upon them…
Etcetera, etcetera…

This poem cries out longingly for a pasquinade:

Make the next line like the last one,
Make the words go bouncing onward,
Make it all go rolling forward,
Keep on writing till you're so bored,
That you're forced to smash the keyboard.

Lewis Carroll wrote a famous pasquinade of "Song of Hiawatha," called "Hiawatha's Photographing." But in my opinion, the best pasquinade of the poem was anonymous. I found it in Carolyn Wells' book, *Parody Anthology*. It is this:

He killed the noble Mudjokivis.
Of the skin he made him mittens,
Made them with the fur side inside,
Made them with the skin side outside.
He, to get the warm side inside,
Put the inside skin side outside;
He, to get the cold side outside,
Put the warm side fur side inside.
That's why he put the fur side inside,
Why he put the skin side outside,
Why he turned them inside outside.

XVIII

WORDS ABOUT WORDS

"A synonym is a word you use when you can't spell the other one." ~ Baltasar Gracián

This group consists of words about words—words like *synonym*, a word having the same meaning as another, or homonym, a word that sounds like another word but has a different meaning. You probably know both these words, but if you're like me, you confuse the two and lose marks in all your English tests. Anyway, the list of ten words here are words that you probably don't know and will never need to know.

Disclaimer: Reading this will not improve your English grades. If you're reading this when you should be doing your homework, then shame on you.

Cohyponyms

There are a lot of words about words with the suffix *nym* (Latin *nym*, word, name) like *synonyms* (words meaning the same but sounding differently) and *homonyms* (words sounding the same but with different meaning). There's *paranym*, which means the same as *euphemism*, but just to confuse everyone there's also *paronym*, which is a homonym wannabe (words that almost sound the same). Consider these two paronyms: *deprecate* and *depreciate*.

This is truly confusing, because these homonym wannabes are also synonym wannabes.

Then there's the *retronym*, recently coined in 1980 by Frank Mankiewicz. It's a desperately useful term that describes words created to supersede other words that have become outdated by events, in order to bring them up to date. So silent movies never became silent movies until the "talkies" were born. And then the talkies soon became just "movies"—so *silent movies* is a retronym.

Retronym has a second and quite different meaning— *words constructed from other words by spelling them backwards*. There are not many such words. One example is provided by *ohm* (a unit of electrical resistance) and its retronym *mho* (a unit of electrical conductance, which is the reciprocal of an ohm). Another and more entertaining example is *coffeeroom* and *mooreeffoc*, the latter word coined by Dickens and explained by G. K. Chesterton as "the queerness of things that have become trite when they are seen suddenly from a new angle."

Also, there's *meronym*, which is a word that refers to something that's part of something else. Thus, a claw is a meronym in respect of a lion.

Related to this is a *hyponym*, which is more particular. It refers to a particular grouping or individual that's part of some more general grouping. For instance, an ocelot is a member of the cat family, *felidae*; *felidae* are mammals; mammals are animals; animals are life forms. Each word is a hyponym of the one that follows, and just to complicate matters each word is also a *hypernym*, of the one that precedes it. A hypernym is a word for a grouping that goes from the general group to the particular—sort of like Russian nesting dolls, only with words.

Finally, this brings us to *cohyponyms*. Cohyponyms are sibling hyponyms. For example, *ocelot* and *puma* are each hyponyms of *felidae*. Together they are cohyponyms.

Logastellus

It's unlikely, I know, but if you really have foresaken your English homework to read this book, then maybe you're a logastellus: a person whose love of words exceeds their knowledge of words. What could be more natural for logastelli than to defer their homework in favor of exposing themselves to new and exciting words, in the hope of leaping the crevasse between their aspirations and their knowledge?

There is a plethora of words for people who are obsessed with words. There's *verbivore*, which has the sense of someone devouring words. There's the logomaniac, who's just mad about words. There's the verbolatrist or grammatolatrist or epeolatrist, all of whom truly worship words. There's the hellomaniac, who is obsessed with foreign or unusual words, and the appalling lexiphanicist, who shows off by the use of an extensive vocabulary. Be warned. If you're a logastellus, you could turn into any one of these word-crazed obsessives.

Onomatophobia

There are far fewer words for those who dislike words than for those who like them. There's the cringing verbophobe who lives in fear of words and that's just about it in terms of general nouns. However, if you have verbophobia, there are varieties of it.

There's *penphobia* or *scriptophobia*, both of which are the morbid fear of writing or of the written word. There's *maledictaphobia*, the fear of saying bad words, which for most people means swear words, although what constitutes a "bad word" is clearly subjective.

Finally there's *onomataphobia*, the fear of hearing a certain word. In most contexts this is likely to pertain to fear of swear words, but not always. An alternative example of onomatophobia was provided by the episode in the

123

British comedy series, *Fawlty Towers*, in which a family of Germans arrives at the hotel and Basil Fawlty (played by John Cleese) becomes obsessed with not talking about "the War."

Morpheme

The morpheme is the linguistic equivalent of the atom in chemistry. Morphemes are the smallest meaningful units in the grammar of a language. Some morphemes are whole words like *the*, *it*, and *each*, but some are prefixes and suffixes, like the *pre* in *prefix* or the *less* in *needless*.

A morpheme is not a syllable. The word *mother*, for example, has two syllables—*mo-ther*—but neither one contains a meaning of its own. Therefore, *mother* is a two-syllable morpheme.

The word *cats*, on the other hand, has one syllable—*cats*—but two morphemes: *cat* and *s*. *Cat* is the animal and *s* is the plural marker. The smallest unit of meaning—*cat*—is contained in a word that means *more than one cat*. Hence, there are two morphemes in the word *cats*.

It's strange that *morpheme* is a paronym with *morphine*. (In case you've forgotten, the paronym is the homonym wannabe—the *almost* homonym.) It's not surprising though. They have the morpheme *morph* in common, because etymologically they derive from the same source. Morpheus was the Greek god of dreams whose name literally means *maker of shapes, shape-shifter, one who can take on many discreet forms*.

The opiate *morphine* got its name because it induces dreams and hallucinations in those who take it. Etymologically it refers to Morpheus's ability to do the same.

Morpheme derives from the god's other ability, that is, to change form—a morpheme being a discreet linguistic form.

124

Metonymy

This literally means *change of name* in Greek and refers to a figure of speech in which one noun or phrase steps in for another. Consider this example: "The Kremlin denied the rumors that there had been an attempted coup." The Kremlin is a building and it couldn't deny any rumors, even if you put a group of journalists in front of it and gave it a megaphone.

As a figure of speech, *metonymy* is thus a kind of symbolism: Buckingham Palace equals Queen Elizabeth II; the White House equals the President; the Death Star equals Darth Vader (or at least it did until his son blew it to smithereens).

In case there should be any confusion, it's worth drawing the distinction between metonymy, metaphor, and euphemism. Metonymy works by the (usually hyperbolic) association between two concepts—people start talking about Darth Vader as though he were the Death Star, instead of the asthmatic guy in a cape who ran the thing.

Metaphor works by similarity and comparison, describing the exploding Death Star, for instance, as "going supernova." Euphemism works by oblique reference, such as calling the Death Star a "planet rearrangement device."

Cruciverbalism

Cruciverbalism is a huge industry that spans the world and consumes the attention of newspaper readers everywhere. Cruciverbalism is the creation of crossword puzzles and the solving of them, which brings great happiness and entertainment to cruciverbalists everywhere. Oh joy!

If I'd never been a cruciverbalist, I would never have discovered that *episcopal* is an anagram of *Pepsi Cola*, or that *East Grinstead* is an anagram of *strangest idea*. Those examples, by the way, come from the London Times Crossword, which is the Mount Everest of crosswords in the U.K., and is distinctively different to The New York Times Crossword, which is the K2 of crosswords in the U.S. And by that metaphor, I mean that The New York Times crossword is just as impossible to climb, given my cruciverbal inadequacies, as the London Times crossword, but in an entirely different way.

Apropos of which, I am obliged to note that, although there are no official rules to cruciverbalism, anyone who uses the many cruciverbal aids on the Internet to help them complete either of these crosswords is no true cruciverbalist.

Sevidical

Okay, I admit it. I was being sevidical, but just as it's possible nowadays to beat a grandmaster at chess by loading a good chess program onto your computer and letting it do the thinking, it's also possible to use Internet thesauri, anagram makers, and word matchers to defeat any well-constructed crossword. Who but a cad would deign to do that?

The true cruciverbal contest is between man (or woman) and crossword—no help from computers or from books. It's just you and your pen against the crossword composer, and may the best cruciverbalist win. *Sevidical*, by the way, means *speaking cruel and harsh words*, but on this topic, I have no doubt that it's justified.

Portmantologist

A portmantologist is someone who studies or coins portmanteau words. A portmanteau word is a word made from the combination of two other words, such as the word *portmanteau* itself. *Portmanteau* is a combination of the French words *porte* and *manteau*, meaning *carry* and *coat* respectively. As a noun, then, *portmanteau* has come to mean *a suitcase—a coat carrier—that opens in two halves*, but in the phrase *portmanteau word,* it refers to a word composed by concatenation and condensation—that is, two words, with elements and meanings of each, packed into one new word.

Commonly used portmanteau words include *smog,* from *smoke* and *fog; motel,* from *motor* and *hotel;* and *brunch,* from *breakfast* and *lunch.* Journalists sometimes coin portmanteau words, as they did with Arnold Schwarzenegger, calling him the *Governator,* a title created from *Governor* and *Terminator.*

The topic of portmanteau words brings to mind the strange breeding that seems to have created the English words *shriek* and *screech. Shriek* comes from the old Nordic *skraekja,* whereas *screech* comes from the Germanic *schrichen.* These words appear somehow to have crossbred to create the two portmanteaus: *shriek* (from *schrichen* with *skraekja*) and *screech* (from *skraekja* with *schrichen*). That's just plain weird.

At the end of this book you will discover a webliography. *Webliography* is also a portmanteau word, invented for the purpose of accurately recording the fact that all the research done in compiling this book was done from web sources. To call a list of such sources a bibliography is more than a misnomer. It's a lie. Hence, this book has a webliography, and I am a portmantologist.

Tmesis

Tmesis refers to the practice of breaking a word in two and inserting another word in the middle. One example is the very British exclamation, "abso-bloody-lutely," which nowadays would probably contain the f-gerund, but otherwise has been in frequent use forever. A U.S. example would be, "boo-freaking-hoo," which was in fashion for a time and probably, more often than not, sported the f-gerund. However, I am trying to limit its appearance here.

The word *tmesis* comes directly from the Greek where it means *a cutting*, which is pleasantly uncomplicated, or it would be if linguists hadn't complicated the topic by describing *tmesis* as a form of infixation.

Infixation is the same as tmesis except for the added nuance that suggests the cutting is done with a firm hand—even vehemence. Thus, "abso-who-cares-lutely" is *tmesis*, but not necessarily *infixation*, because the substitution of "who cares" for "bloody" lessens, rather than increases, the enthusiasm with which the word is split.

We can further complicate this topic by introducing the thorny little problem of the split infinitive. *Star Trek* was a great TV series in its day, but it horrified grammarians everywhere, because it dared to boldly split infinitives that no man had ever split before. Worse than that, it did so before an audience of millions of school children whose grammatical habits a whole generation of English teachers was trying to nurture. However, the question deserves to be asked: What's so un-bloody-grammatical about splitting infinitives?

Well, truth to bloody-well tell, splitting infinitives is equivalent to tmesis, and tmesis was once frowned on as an improper usage favored by the lower classes—from whom one would expect such shoddy word play.

Early English grammarians believed that, because the Romans and Greeks didn't split infinitives, we shouldn't either. In taking this stance, grammarians blithely ignore the fact that neither the Romans nor the Greeks had two-word infinitives.

Sadly, the early English grammarians had a fixation about infixation.

Hypozeuxis

Hypozeuxis is the literary or rhetorical technique in which a set of parallel clauses (or sentences) is created for a specific effect. This is what's going on in the first three lines of this verse from Alfred, Lord Tennyson's poem, "The Charge of the Light Brigade."

> Cannon to right of them,
> Cannon to left of them,
> Cannon behind them
> Volley'd and thunder'd;
> Storm'd at with shot and shell,
> While horse and hero fell,
> They that had fought so well
> Came thro' the jaws of Death
> Back from the mouth of Hell,
> All that was left of them,
> Left of six hundred.

Winston Churchill used hypozeuxis in his famous radio address: "We shall fight on the beaches. We shall fight on the landing grounds. We shall fight in the fields and in the streets. We shall fight in the hills. We shall never surrender!"

The deliberate use of repetition is powerful, powerful, powerful.

XIX

DIRTY WORDS

"Men are not ashamed to think something dirty, but they are ashamed when they imagine that others might believe them capable of these dirty thoughts." ~ Friedrich Nietzsche

I really should warn you before you start reading this chapter that it's all about smut. It is all about dirty words and, not just dirty words, but dirty words that are used to describe smut and horribly smutty things.

I'm reasonably certain what has happened here. You've stumbled across this page accidentally, and you're already feeling a little embarrassed that you're here. Well, don't worry. Just open the book somewhere else, and you'll find some much more respectable words than those below. Sorry about that…and *sayonara*.

You're still reading this? In which case you must be one of the few readers that actually has an interest in *spurcitious* language. Well, I'm sorry to disappoint you, but didn't you read the title of this book? It is *Words You Don't Know*. If you're looking for someone who writes dirty, you've come to the right place.

Unfortunately, you've also come to the wrong place, because the words you're going to read here may well be dirty, but like the word *spurcitious*—which means *foul or obscene*—you haven't met with these words before. So I doubt if you are going to find this a satisfying experience.

And if by some small chance you actually have met with these words before, then I can only say that I'm deeply impressed—also a little creeped out, to be honest. But how could I not be impressed with someone who has pursued smut so fervently that they know even the obscure words that appear on these pages. So let's see how creepy…I mean impressive…you really are. Test yourself. Here's a list of ten.

Fescennine

Well? Have you seen this one before? It's an adjective. It means *smutty, obscene, lewd, licentious* and even *scurrilous*. In fact, it means pretty much the same as *spurcitious*. It refers to all the words in which you are so obviously showing an unhealthy interest.

Aischrolatry

I write this rather tentatively, but it seems obvious to me that there are some people who appreciate smut. You know as well as I do that I wouldn't have written this if I didn't recognize that fact. I'm a writer, ferchrissake, and the whole point of writing is readership. I know damn well that there are people out there who don't object to smut. There are some who even like it. I've been told that there are one or two who even deign to visit pornographic web sites, and beyond that, there are some who are aischrolatrists—people who really like smut, people who worship smut.

Coprolalia

Remember when you were a little kid and you were trying out your first dirty words? Maybe you were on the playground at school or at a neighbor's house when you let loose with a string of fescennine descriptors for your playmate. And do you remember the schoolteacher or the priggish mother next door who stood over you, shaking her finger in your face, and saying that she would not tolerate such filthy language in her classroom / house? Well, here you are all those years later, and you're reading a chapter on dirty words. I'd say her suspicions about you were spot on.

I'm no expert in this area of study, but I suspect that most aischrolatrists are coprolaliacs—people who use foul, obscene or scatological language uncontrollably. I'm not much of a psychologist, but I suspect that admiring smut and using smutty language go together quite nicely. The way I see it, most aischrolatrists have an unhealthy attachment to coprophemia (*obscene language*).

Borborygmite

And if those aischrolatrists do have such a putative attachment, then I can confidently classify them as borborygmites. The word *borborygmite*, I believe, derives from the word *borborygmus*, which means nothing more indelicate than the *rumbling of gas in the stomach*, a condition that we all (with the obvious exception of HRH, Queen Elizabeth II) suffer from on occasion. *Borborygmus* is not a foul word and yet *borborygmite* is as foul as it sounds. It means *a person who, contrary to all dictates of civilized behavior, is practiced in the use of coprophemia*.

Pareunia

Beyond the purely scatological, which I've decided to exclude here in the interests of good taste, most coprophemia relates directly or indirectly to pareunia. And by pareunia, I mean amphigony. And by amphigony, I mean gamogenesis. I'm sure you're catching my drift here. Just as there are many, many slang words for fornication, there are also a great many obscure words for fornication.

Varietist

If you're a confirmed aischrolatrist, then you have probably lost your interest in straight sex. Most likely your tastes are, let us say, more inclusive, broader, more eclectic, possibly more specific, certainly undiscriminating, or…just plain weird.

That would make you a varietist—one who has unorthodox sexual practices—by which I mean a *pervert*. But *varietist* is a much nicer word, don't you agree?

Catamite

Don't get the idea that a nicer word necessarily indicates nicer behavior. (We both know from our coprolalia example that it's unlikely to be the case.) I've been told, for instance, that there are some varietists who are wont to keep a catamite.

Zeus, for example, had a catamite named Ganymede. Zeus was an inveterate varietist. He spotted the handsome, young Ganymede herding his flock on Mount Ida. As was his wont, Zeus swooped down onto Mount Ida in the form of an eagle and carried Ganymede off to Mount Olympus where he became Zeus' cupbearer. It always gets complicated when gods do things like that and this was no exception.

Ganymede's father, King Laomedon of Troy, grieved so terribly for his lost son, that Zeus sent Hermes to him with a gift of a golden vine and two swift horses that could run over water. Laomedon apparently accepted the gesture as compensation, and that might have settled the matter were it not for Zeus' eternally jealous and intrusive wife.

Hera was outraged at Zeus' varietism when she heard that Ganymede was not just Zeus's cupbearer, but also his lover, and she proceeded to give Zeus a piece of her mind.

Presumably to flaunt his complete lack of regard for her opinion, Zeus placed Ganymede's image amongst the stars in the form of the constellation Aquarius, the water carrier, or cupbearer, or, if you like, catamite.

As a point of law, keeping a catamite—that is, keeping a young boy for the purposes of sex—is not legal in any place I know of, except Mount Olympus, where they seem to make up their own rules.

Thygatrilagnia

Thygatrilagnia, an incestuous desire for one's daughter, is not exactly illegal, but doing anything about it certainly is. This is true in most places except for Mount Olympus, where—as we've seen—just about anything goes. The same is true of adelphepothia, an incestuous desire for one's sister; adelphirexia, an incestuous desire for one's nephew; and adelphithymia, an incestuous desire for one's niece.

As far as I know, these are the only dirty words that specifically deal with incest. The sad fact is that you can have incestuous desires for any other relative and you will not be able to sum up your feelings in a single word.

Oh, the paucity of our language!

Renifleur

If you really want dirty then, in my book, a renifleur is dirty. A renifleur is someone who gets sexual pleasure from body smells. How foul is that?

Well, I suppose I could have sold it a little better.

The definition is non-specific as regards which smells turn a renifleur on, therefore I could have presented a renifleur as a person who responds positively to pheromones. However, we both know that whoever invented that word didn't have pheromones in mind. A renifleur is just another dirty rotten varietist.

135

Tribadism

And finally, we come to tribadism, which is no longer as disapproved of as it once was. In fact, it's not really a dirty word. It's just a sexual preference. In many countries, tribades are allowed their sexual leanings as never before. It's even legal in several states in America (also in the U.K.) for tribades to marry.

The word *tribade* comes from the Ancient Greek verb *tribein*, which means *to rub*, and a tribade is a lesbian. The word *lesbian* itself derives from the fact that the Greek poetess Sappho lived on the island of Lesbos and wrote poems that spoke of love and sexuality between women. Because of that, the inhabitants of Lesbos, Lesbians, were all tarred with the same sexual brush for decades—something that annoys them to this day and has them calling themselves Lesbosians.

We could fix this sorry situation by reverting to the word *tribade* and letting Lesbos have its word back. But you know that's never going to happen.

XX

SWEAR WORDS AND
CURSE WORDS

"Oaths are but words, and words but wind."
~ Samuel Butler

Warning: To write about swear words and curse words you don't know, I actually have to use the words and the words they allude to, otherwise we'd be swimming and soon drowning in euphemisms. This chapter is full of—surprise!— offensive words. For the sake of those with a sensitive nature, I have chosen to use these words only where I consider it necessary to their nature. Elsewhere I have resorted to terms such as f-word, s-word, *etc. Anyway, you have been warned!*

The word *swear* has two meanings, or at least it seems that way. *Swearing*, as in "swearing an oath," means *making a solemn promise*, and *swearing* also means *using foul language*. The two meanings are closely related since the swearing of an oath traditionally involved swearing on the Bible or in God's name. So when, in the 16th century, people developed a habit of invoking "sacred names" when no oath was being made, they were guilty of "taking sacred names in vain." Such an act was profane (the opposite of sacred) and the word used to describe such a horrendous sin was profanity.

Honestly, I think it was inevitable that this habit would arise. The Ten Commandments almost certainly guaranteed that the human race would eventually start swearing like mad. Nothing tempts us sinners to "shalt" like a stern "shalt not..."

The same applies to cursing, since cursing traditionally involved invoking sacred or demonic entities by name, and enlisting their assistance in causing bad things to rain down upon the person cursed. So inappropriate cursing is also profanity.

Here is a list of ten words that you've probably not met with before, which relate to swear words and curse words.

Etymon

As a general rule, swearing of any kind is frowned on in polite society and has been through the ages. So there is a tendency to invent euphemisms for swear words in order that they might be used in a milder form. In the Middle Ages, the fashion was to use nonsense or vaguely sound-alike words as substitutes for sacred names. That produced religious swear words like *egad* and *zounds*. *Egad* was a simple substitute for *God*. *Zounds* was a short-ening of *God's wounds*, as was—excuse my French—*woun-dikins*. *Odds bodkins* stood in for *God's body*, and *gadzooks* was *God's hooks*, referring to the nails used in crucifixion.

You might think that the creation of such religious swear words has stopped, but it hasn't. The newer ones simply don't sound so archaic. *Gee whiz* and *jeez* (for *Jesus*) are quite recent, as are: *jeepers creepers* (for *Jesus Christ*), *doggone* (for *God damn*), *gosh* or *golly* (for *God*) and *great scott* (for *good God*). Also recent is the use of the names *Christopher Columbus*, *Judas Priest* and *Jiminy Cricket* as mild swear words for which the etymon is *Jesus Christ*. An etymon, by the way, is a root word from which other words derive, and etymology is, of course, the study of etymons.

Execration

To most people, the use of such religious swear words is now regarded as tame and has no real place in execration, execration being the act of cursing, the curse itself, as well as the thing that is cursed or loathed. When you really want to express yourself by cursing, obscure Christian euphemisms no longer cut the mustard. However, direct curses are rarely offensive in the words they employ, since the whole point is to wish ill on someone rather than deliver a spirited insult.

Take for example the Chinese curse: "May you come to the attention of the authorities!" It may sound a little lame at first blush, but that's probably because a certain amount of bile has been lost in translation. I'm told by U.S. tax evaders that "May you come to the attention of the IRS!" is about as mean as a curse can get. Even so, it doesn't have the poetic grit of my favorite Arab curse: "May wild asses defile the grave of your grandmother!" Neither does it have the surreal spitefulness of my favorite Irish curse: "May the seven terriers of hell sit on the spool of your breast and bark in at your soul-case!"

Cambronne

"That's a load of old cambronne"—a phrase that used to be heard in the tearooms and coffee houses of 19th century England when someone doubted the veracity of an idea or opinion. Sadly, it has fallen into disuse and lives on only in footnotes to treatises on latrinalia (the definition of which is discussed later in this chapter). The word *cambronne* is eponymous as every Frenchman surely knows. Here's one version of its origin:

The scene is the final hours of the battle of Waterloo and the French General Pierre Cambronne finds himself heavily outnumbered and surrounded by English soldiers and cannon. In command of the British troops is the generous

General Colville. Through his young interpreter, Charles Bartleby-Snobsworth, Colville calls to Cambronne with the words: "I say, old boy, no need for any further nastiness. Why not lay down your weapons and we can all watch the rest of the pyrotechnics from here?"

General Colville unfortunately cannot speak a word of French, and Bartleby-Snobsworth, the interpreter, actually skipped French classes at Eton to play Cricket, so he knows only *"un mot où deux."* General Cambronne, who speaks flawless English, chooses foolishly to respond in French, shouting out bravely, *"La garde meurt et ne se rend pas!"*

Bartleby-Snobsworth doesn't understand a word of this and mishears it anyway, thinking Cambronne said, *"merde,"* not *"meurt."* So when Colville asks him what Cambronne said, he replies, "Shit, sir! The Frenchy said 'shit'." "That's hardly polite," mutters General Colville as he signals the order to fire the cannons.

That's one version of what happened at Waterloo and it's a load of old cambronne, but the fact is that no one seems to know the truth. After-battle commentary had two versions: Cambronne saying, *"Merde!"* and Cambronne saying, *"La garde meurt et ne se rend pas!"* ("The Guard dies and does not surrender!").

Cambronne, who survived but was wounded, denied saying either of these things. Nevertheless, *merde* became known in France as *le mot Cambronne* and, in Britain, *cambronne* became an eponymous euphemism.

Quadriliteral

"Good authors, too, who once knew better words,
Now only use four-letter words. Writing prose...
Anything goes."

Or at least that's what the lyrics of the Cole Porter song will insist. However, quadriliterals—those four letter words—are still largely avoided in many situations. The f-word, king of the quadriliterals, was in common usage in the 16th century and only became a vulgar term in the 18th century—banned even from the *Oxford English Dictionary*. It was outlawed in print in England by the Obscene Publications Act of 1857, and in the U.S. by the Comstock Act of 1873. The censorship didn't persist, however, because writers trying to portray realistic speech saw the need to use the f-word.

The American author, Norman Mailer, tried in 1948 to reintroduce the word in his novel, *The Naked and the Dead*. His publisher, however, prevailed upon him to replace the offensive quadriliteral with the word *fug* throughout. When, at some later date, Mailer was introduced to fellow writer Dorothy Parker, she greeted him with, "So you're the man who can't spell *fuck*."

By 1950, James Jones's *From Here to Eternity* was published with the inclusion of 50 instances of the f-word. By the time the 1960s came around, the f-word was slipping past the U.K. and U.S. censors on a regular basis, and Kenneth Tynan, the English theatre critic, made a name for himself worldwide by becoming the first person to use the questionable quadriliteral on live television.

Hadeharia

My parents informed me at an early age that the word *fuck*, the king of the quadriliterals, was strictly taboo and never to be uttered. When I was growing up, I spent many (many, many, many) hours laboring alongside a bunch of down-to-earth shipyard welders whose use of the word *fuck* as a verb was pretty much non-stop and liberally mixed with the word as just about every other part of speech or usage you can think of—noun, adjective, adverb, and gerund—even tmesis. I estimated at the time that the word *fuck* made up about 10 percent of all the words that came out of their mouths. They had even developed inventive usages like compound words and portmanteau words, my favorites being *fuckworthy* and *fucktard*. Really creative guys, those welders. But then, it was Liverpool, and that's just how Liverpudlian welders roll.

Later on in life, when I saw *Reservoir Dogs* at the movies, I realized that Quentin Tarantino must have run into exactly the same group of welders. I'd love to find a word that describes the habit of constantly using the word *fuck*, but I don't think there is one. However, I did find *hadeharia*, which means *the constant use of the word* hell. Sadly, I've never met a hadeharian. I presume the word dates back to the time when *hell* was consider a strong word and *Hades*, the Greek underworld, was a common euphemism.

But I am undaunted. In the spirit of creativity, I hearby propose this new word—*fuckharia*—to honor all my one-time fuckharian colleagues. But not that fugharian, Norman Mailer.

Lalochezia

Lalochezia is the use of foul or abusive language in response to sudden stress or pain. It's a quirk of many people, in my experience—with the most common expletive being the s-word or the f-word. However, lalochezia need not be confined to such unimaginative expletives. It can be flowery.

I remember, for example, a relative of mine who was working on a boat engine one day. He pushed down too hard on a wrench, which promptly slipped off the bolt it was gripping, and this caused him to smash his hand into the engine casing. "You snot-gobbling bastard!" he screamed at the motor, which struck me as delightfully inappropriate.

My mother, from whom I never heard a single swear word in my life, was inclined to simply shout "Damn! Damn! Damn!" when pain moved her to explete. Very mild indeed, but at least it was a quadriliteral. In any event, from my observations, euphemisms seem to work just as well as the foulest of language. I remember a very polite aunt of mine shouting "Sugar! Sugar! Sugar! Sugar! Sugar!" when her hammer hit her thumb and then muttering "sugar" under her breath when she realized I was watching her.

Personally, my habit is to make a lot of noise. Indeed, it seems quite inappropriate to me to try to articulate anything in response to unwelcome intense sensory stimuli. So, I just scream my heart out.

Latrinalia

The c-word is undoubtedly the queen of all swear words and, as in the game of chess, the queen is more powerful than the king, at least in its ability to offend.

It wasn't always like that. Most people will be surprised to discover that London once boasted a district called Gropecunte Lane, named in honor of the prostitutes that worked there. When Londoners eventually decided that a name change was in order, they decided on the euphemism Threadneedle Street so that the essential character of the locale would not be lost.

This is the street on which the Bank of England was eventually built and, oddly, the Bank of England became affectionately known as "The Old Lady of Threadneedle Street." However, that title was not in honor of any of the ladies who were affectionately known for having their needles threaded prior to the appearance of the bank. It was to honor the memory of Sarah Whitehead whose brother Philip, a former employee of the bank, was executed for the crime of forgery. This caused poor Sarah to lose her mind and, after his execution, she turned up at the bank asking for him every day for 25 years, until she died of old age.

Latrinalia, as you may be able to deduce from its etymons, refers to words that, like the c-word, are fit only for restroom walls. Attempts have been made to return the c-word to common usage, or if not entirely common usage, to a less offensive status. Several novelists have tried to habituate censors to its use in literature in recent times. James Joyce included it once in *Ulysses*; D. H. Lawrence used the word ten times in *Lady Chatterley's Lover*, thus prompting a famous British obscenity trial; and Samuel Beckett used it once in *Malone Dies*.

Well, after these literary forays failed, the British punk band, The Sex Pistols, picked up the gauntlet, making a spirited attempt to promote the word with the song, "Pretty Vacant," with the word *vacant* being pronounced *vay-kunt*, as in "we're vacant...and we don't care."

The Sex pistols were in excellent literary company with Joyce, Lawrence and Beckett, but their efforts failed. Bringing the c-word into common usage was something that was beyond even Shakespeare. He referred to the word obliquely in the play, *Twelfth Night.* In the scene where Malvolio scrutinizes a letter for signs that the handwriting is indeed Olivia's, he says, "These be her very c's, her u's, 'n' her t's, and thus she makes her great p's."

Despite all of these artistic efforts, the c-word remains unchallenged as the most obscene of all words. If one were to bring it into common usage, we'd need to find another word to occupy its disquieting throne.

Dysphemism

The abusive British word *berk* is a euphemism for the c-word. It comes from cockney rhyming slang, *berk* being short for Berkshire Hunt. *Oxford* is another euphemism with a rhyming slang origin; it is short for "Oxford punt."

Other non-rhyming slang euphemisms include the *velvet glove*, the *oval office* and the *sausage wallet*. There are many more. Euphemisms grow wild in the field of latrinology, but dysphemisms are less common.

A dysphemism is the opposite of a euphemism. It refers to the deliberate use of a more, rather than a less, vulgar term. A simple example would be to call someone a fuckwit rather than a fool. The meaning is the same, but the word used is somewhat more expressive.

It's interesting that some apparent dysphemisms are, technically, not dysphemisms at all. The word *cock-up*, for instance, derives from the brewer's practice of turning the spigot—or cock—of a barrel upwards if the beer inside had spoiled.

If you choose to describe a fool as a prick rather than a fuckwit, you might believe you're inferring that he's a penis. That's the common belief, but the derivation is otherwise. It harks back to the early days of agriculture and the farming equipment used to yoke oxen to ploughs (*plows* for American English speakers). A shaft of sharpened wood, called a prick, was used to keep the oxen in place. If the oxen didn't pull as directed, the prick dug into them. Kicking against the prick, as oxen sometimes did, thus became a metaphor for resisting authority stupidly.

In the U.K., the French Connection, a chain of boutiques, hit on the idea of re-branding itself as French Connection UK, or FCUK for short. To my mind, that counts as a deliberate dysphemism. Nevertheless, it turned out to be a fcuking brilliant marketing ploy that attracted more than a little attention—especially when they came out with their eau de toilette, which they called simply, "FCUK Her."

Grawlix

Grawlixes are typographical symbols that appear in dialogue balloons in graphical comics to indicate that some swear word or other is implied. The term was coined by Mort Walker, the Beetle Bailey cartoonist, after he'd been employing grawlixes for a while. As a grawlix, the f-word becomes something like f@&#. And if you want to be less specific about which unacceptably offensive word you are using, you can simply plump for something like *$&#%!

This is not the only strategy available for partially censoring words. You can modify the words with asterisks, as in *"what the f***,"* or disemvowel them, as in *"what the fck,"* or resort to abbreviation, as in *"WTF."* You can substitute a euphemism, like *effing* or *freaking*—but please, in deference to Dorothy Parker, not *fugging*.

There's also bleeping, as in "Why don't you take a flying *bleep* at a rolling doughnut?" This technique is often used for text that is intended to be read aloud. However, as the example demonstrates, with bleeping you can easily lose a very effective alliteration.

Apropos of which, the *flying fuck* is not a meaningless poetic idea. In earlier times, it was a term used to describe having sex on horseback while the horse was in motion and, thus, gaining entry to the 5-Foot High Club.

Scatolinguistics

Scatolinguistics started out as meaning *the study of words related to excrement*. The word was coined by James McCawley, an influential linguist and, for much of his life, professor of linguistics at the University of Chicago. He wrote his cromulent scatolinguistic treatises under the pseudonyms of Quang Phuc Dong and Yuck Foo of the nonexistent South Hanoi Institute of Technology. For want of appropriate terms, *scatolinguistics* has now come to mean *the study of the etymology and usage of all vulgar and profane expressions.*

To my mind, there ought to be a special subset within the broader area of study for the distinction between British and American profanity. In some places the words are identical, which is fine, but there are jarring differences. For example, *fanny* in America is a mild alternative to *ass* (buttocks), whereas in the U.K. it is schizophrenic. It's a less offensive alternative for the c-word when it is referring to the female parts, but it's completely inoffensive slang when it means *spending time ineffectively,* as in *fannying around.*

The British commonly use both *wanker* and *tosser* as insults (meaning *masturbator*). Neither word is used in America, although the word *jackoff* is used, but with much less frequency.

The British don't use *motherfucker,* which has to do with tradition. African slaves coined the word to describe the slave owners who raped their mothers.

While Americans are likely to say *buck-* or *butt-naked,* the British equivalent is *bollock-naked or stark bollock-naked.* Americans say *bullshit* when Brits would say *bollocks.* The word *bollocks* is from the Old English word *beallucas,* meaning *testicles.* One can only assume that the word *bollocks* was regarded as offensive to high-minded Protestants and, for that reason, didn't make it onto the Mayflower.

XXI

INSULTING WORDS

"Sticks and stones will break my bones, but names will never hurt me." ~ Anonymous

That's what we used to chant as kids when we got into name-calling contests in the schoolyard. Of course, it's untrue and it's disingenuous. It implies that the name callers are pursuing a stupid strategy when, in truth, the right insult is deeply wounding.

Consider, for example, the American actress, Jean Harlow. At dinner with Dame Margot Asquith, the wife of British Prime Minister Herbert Asquith, the actress kept pronouncing Dame Asquith's name as "Mar-got," rather than "Mar-go," as it should be pronounced. Eventually Dame Asquith corrected her with the immortal words: "No Jean, the T is silent, as in Harlow." Being insulted brutally is bad enough, but being insulted famously is far worse.

Nevertheless, Jean Harlow escaped lightly when compared to Lord Castlereagh, a despised British politician, who was held responsible for the massacre at St. Peter's Fields, where British cavalry charged into a crowd of 80,000 protesters, killing 15 and wounding hundreds.

Castlereagh resigned in the wake of this atrocity, lived the remainder of his life a broken man, and eventually committed suicide. But even in death he was reviled.

Byron wrote the only epitaph for Lord Castlereagh that anyone ever remembers. It's this:

> Posterity will ne'er survey
> A nobler scene than this.
> Here lie the bones of Castlereagh.
> Stop, traveller, and piss.

This four-line poem distills the essence of insult. A good insult makes no apology for itself. It is dressed to kill and performs accordingly. English is rich with insulting words, and there can be no surprise that many have lapsed into obscurity as other, newer words have edged them out of common usage. Nevertheless, some of them can surely be revived if enough of us employ them whenever there is an opportunity. Here are ten:

Jementous

An effective means of insulting someone is to accuse them of polluting the air, as in: "People fell at his feet, but only after they'd smelt his breath." If the occasion warrants it, you might try: "Your aftershave's distinctive. Do I detect a hint of hircismus?" *Hircismus* has two related meanings: *offensive armpit odor* and *the smell of a goat*. *Jementous* is similar. It's an adjective that means *smelling of horse urine*, and it may catch people unawares, because it doesn't sound like an insult (at least not to me).

As few of us spend much time in the company of horses, you may no longer appreciate the distinctive nature of this insult, but, if you've read *The Tempest* by Shakespeare, you'll have no doubt of the putative unpleasantness of the odor. In *The Tempest*, Trinculo addresses Caliban (the oafish monster) with the words: "Monster, I do smell all horse-piss, at which my nose is in great indignation." Caliban was obviously jementous.

150

Slubberdegullion

This word is superior to *jementous* from the onomato-poeic perspective. It really does sound like a damning insult and it is. A slubberdegullion is a slobbering foul individual, a worthless sloven, a pigpen, a jeeter, a tramp, an uncouth slob, a disgusting draggletail, and a torpid and tawdry tatterdemalion. This is someone who lives in the gutter and whose only function on this planet is to serve as a warning to others. The origin of *slubberdegullion* is uncompromising: *slubber,* from the Dutch, means *to daub* or *to smear*, and *degullion* is a corruption of the Old French *de goalon* meaning a *sloven*. A slubberdegullion is a slob.

Helminth

It's no compliment to call someone a slubberdegullion, but it is quite a mild insult when compared to something like *helminth*. A helminth is an intestinal worm. It's the same as the difference (in the U.S.) between calling someone a doofus and calling someone a dipshit. Or if you prefer a U.K. example, it's the difference between a plonker and a complete fuckwit.

As an epithet, *helminth* can be classified with cockroach, slug, leech, dung beetle and other lowlife for which we have no love. However, the word's onomatopoeic qualities are superior to slubberdegullion, and it bests all other lowlife nouns I've run across. It's a truly great insult—so much so that I recommend that you find someone you truly dislike and deploy it immediately.

Excerebrose

Perhaps the greatest insult of all in our society is to proclaim that someone is utterly stupid. There is a treasury of insults of this type in circulation, of which the following serve as excellent examples:

- He's not letting his education get in the way of his ignorance.
- He's so stupid he uses two hands to eat with chopsticks.
- They shot him through the stupid forest, and he didn't miss a tree.
- He's as sharp as a bowling ball.
- He has too much yardage between the goal posts.
- He is two socks short of a pair.
- When you look into his eyes, you see the back of his head.
- He's nobody's fool, but we're hoping someone will adopt him.
- He's missing a few buttons on his remote.
- He's so dumb he wouldn't pass a blood test.
- His incompetence is an inspiration to morons everywhere.
- He doesn't have all his cornflakes in one box.
- He's all foam and no beer.
- The cheese fell off his cracker.
- He couldn't pour water out of a boot with instructions on the heel.
- His intellect is rivaled only by garden tools.
- His elevator doesn't go all the way to the top floor.
- The wheel's still spinning but the hamster's dead.

Likewise there are many words that simply mean *idiot*, including less common ones such as: *dummkopf, jabberknowl, balatron, ninnyhammer, gowk (or gawk), schnook* and *nincompoop*.

There are probably many others. *Excerebrose* is more precise than any of these, and in my view, to be preferred. It simply and literally means *brainless*.

Aeolist

"The age of chivalry is past. Bores have succeeded to dragons," said Benjamin Disraeli.

So perhaps the heroes of our day are those who slay the bores who encroach on our lives. Boredom, it seems, is the blight of our gadget-strewn age and something that deeply offends us. Lisa Kirk observed sagely and savagely, "A gossip is one who talks to you about others; a bore is one who talks to you about himself; and a brilliant conversationalist is one who talks to you about yourself."

An aeolist is thus highly offensive, since an aeolist is not just a pompous bore, but also one who pretends to be inspired. The self-flattering aeolist is a bore by commission, by exhibition, and by definition. If you wish to accuse someone of being a bore, then *aeolist* is the insult of choice.

Cacafuego

A cacafuego is an outrageous bore rather than an affected, pompous bore. So *cacafuego* is a nice counterpoint to *aeolist* and should be used when you run into an out-and-out braggart—someone who is full of braggadocio and wishes to shower you in it.

Cacafuego translates directly from the Spanish compound word made up of *shit* and *fire*, and is, thus, nicely unambiguous and easy to remember. Should you run into a cacafuego and you just can't bring the word to mind, call him *shitfire*. It works just as well.

Scullion

"I am His Majesty's dog at Kew. Pray, tell me sir, whose dog are you?"

Insults that are aimed directly at rank or position, as satirized in that quotation, are no longer as common as they once were. *Scullion* is an example. It is anachronistic because it means *a low-ranking domestic servant who performs menial kitchen tasks*. The word comes from the Old French *escouillon*, which meant a *swab* or *cloth*.

Shakespeare used *scullion* as an insult in *Henry IV Part 2*, with Falstaff saying to Mistress Quickly, "Away, you scullion! You rampallian! You fustilarian! I'll tickle your catastrophe." (For the record a rampallian is a mean wretch and a fustilarian is a scoundrel.) Nevertheless, despite its Shakespearean lineage, *scullion* doesn't pack much of a punch. We're all scullions of a kind these days, and anyway, remember Cinderella? She was a scullion and she did almost as well as Eva Peron.

Pygalgia

The medical profession has many entertaining words for "pain in the ass" and *pygalgia* is perhaps the best by virtue of being easy to remember—just think *pig* and *algia*. For that reason it comes out ahead of *coccydynia* (*a pain in the coccyx*, to be accurate, but so close to the ass as makes no difference), *proctalgia* (*a pain in the rectal muscle*) and *rectalgia* (*a pain in the rectum*). Technically, pygalgia is actually a pain in the buttocks, but if you're delivering an insult you probably don't care much for the technicalities. If *pygalgia* appeals to you, then you'll probably go for *steatopygous*, which is the medical term for a *lard ass* (or lard arse). And just so you have the complete collection, the medical profession also gives us *ankyloproctia*, which is the condition of having a constricted anus—as in "he's so tight-assed that, if he ate coal, he'd shit diamonds."

Poltroon

If you want to call someone a coward and you've grown tired of using worn-out insults like *yellowbelly* and *chicken*, then *poltroon* is an excellent substitute. The word comes originally from the Italian *poltrone*, which meant both *lazy fellow* and *coward*. In fact *poltrone* may have been the Old Italian word for *couch potato*, since the Italian *poltro* means *couch*. However, as it morphed its way through French into English, the cowardly aspect of its meaning was emphasized.

There are a few other obscure words that you might also be tempted to use. There's *milquetoast*, which is eponymous, dating back Caspar Milquetoast, a meek, unassertive cartoon character created by H. T. Webster in 1924. There's also *caitiff*, which has the same etymology as the word *captive* and means *a despicably mean and cowardly person*. And there's *dastard*, from which we get *dastardly*, which *means cowardly, but also sly and cunning*. *Poltroon* is less ambiguous than these options and, to my mind, more impressive. I heartily recommend it for addressing all the cowards you encounter.

Clapperdudgeon

This qualifies as my favorite insult because it's completely off the wall. A clapperdudgeon is a beggar whose parents were beggars. A clapperdudgeon is not just a bum, deadbeat, mendicant, hobo, panhandling vagabond, but someone who is skilled in a trade proudly handed down from father to son and from mother to son.

There are probably even clapperdudgeons whose parents were clapperdudgeons. They're not just beggars. They are quintessentially beggars. They are the essence of beggardom.

That's pretty darn insulting.

XXII

LEGAL WORDS YOU DON'T KNOW

*"The answer to this last question will determine whether you
are drunk or not: Was Mickey Mouse a cat or a dog?"*
~ Police officer to driver, recorded on police
car video during traffic stop

From insults, to injury. What better topic to follow our
chapter on insults than a chapter on legal words?

It is curious that there are so many television programs
concerned entirely with the practice of law. It's easy to
understand why there are so many dramas involving the
emergency services (the cops, firefighters, and doctors),
because their activities are associated with responses to
crises, and drama naturally surrounds the events they
deal with.

The law is different. The law presents a fundamental
philosophical quest: the pursuit of truth and justice. So
in TV programs, the legal profession tends to be lionized,
usually held up as a paragon of virtue and dedicated to
the quest.

Yet in reality, that awkwardly complex world outside
the TV, the legal profession is rarely loved and often
deeply disrespected. This is to some degree reflected in
the following ten obscure words that relate to the legal
profession.

Grimgribber

A grimgribber is a lawyer or attorney or solicitor. The term solicitor, by the way, is chiefly British. In America, *solicitor* usually denotes someone who directly seeks donations or desires to trade goods or services, such as a sales rep or a prostitute—or a lawyer. In Britain, solicitors aren't allowed to advertise or directly solicit work, so naturally they are called solicitors. The meaning of *grimgribber* was originally *legal jargon*, but the term also came to embrace those who trade in it, until, sadly, it fell out of common usage. It is, in my opinion, a much more apposite word than *lawyer*, *solicitor* or *attorney* can ever hope to be.

According to the American Bar Association there are currently around 1.1 million grimgribbers practicing in the United States. That means one grimgribber for every 265 people. The typical U.S. grimgribber is Caucasian (90 percent) and male (75 percent). New York and California are the states with the highest number of grimgribbers, each with about 100,000 or so.

It's widely and wrongly believed that America has about 70 percent of all the world's grimgribbers. Despite the fact that it is the most litigious country in the world, that suggestion is wide of the truth. Brazil has a grimgribber for every 326 Brazilians; New Zealand has one for every 391; Spain one for every 395. And so on. If you take the top 7 grimgribberish countries, the U.S. has about 50 percent of the grimgribbers. If you keep on adding countries to the list, you soon encounter India with 1 million grimgribbers, many of whom are eager to provide grimgribbing services to the U.S. It's doubtful whether the U.S. has even 25 percent the world's grimgribbers.

Tortfeaser

Most of the legal shows on TV are about grimgribbers and tortfeasers. The one that set the standard for others to follow was "Perry Mason." Perry would normally find himself in court defending some putative tortfeaser, someone who was accused of "murder with malice afore-thought." With a little bit of research into the circumstances and a clever approach to cross-examination, this giant of a grimgribber would prove that the real tortfeaser was someone else entirely. Justice would thus be done and the person wrongly accused of tortfeasing would breathe a sigh of relief. That kind of thing happens quite often in TV land and almost never in real life. A tortfeaser is, by the way, a wrongdoer.

Snollygoster

A snollygoster is a shrewd but unprincipled individual. The word is sometimes rightly used to describe grimgribbers and politicians, but often applies equally to plaintiffs who bring unreasonable lawsuits and, as it sometimes happens, win them.

The most famous of these wheel-of-fortune lawsuits was undoubtedly that brought by 81-year-old Stella Liebeck. In 1994, she sued McDonald's (the hamburger chain) after she spilled a cup of McDonald's coffee on herself, suffering third-degree burns to her legs, groin, and buttocks. A New Mexico jury awarded her $2.9 million in damages. She thus gave her name to the Stella Awards, which regularly highlight the most egregious legal snollygosting of the previous year.

Despite this eponymity, it only seems fair to include other details of Stella Liebeck's case. McDonald's managers specified that its coffee should be served at 180-190 degrees Fahrenheit; liquids at that temperature can cause third-degree burns in 2-7 seconds. The resultant scarring is typically permanent and McDonald's did not provide any warning of the possible danger. Following the initial award of $2.7 million in punitive damages and a further

$200,000 in compensatory damages, the total award was actually reduced to $640,000 and, ultimately, Lieback and McDonalds entered into a secret settlement rather than pursue the case through the court of appeal.

But here is perhaps the most important point: The U.S. National Coffee Association recommends that coffee be brewed at "between 195-205 degrees Fahrenheit for optimal extraction." If it is not drunk immediately, it should be "maintained at 180-185 degrees Fahrenheit." So really, what did McDonald's do wrong?

Another famous snollygosting tale is provided by Mr. Merv Grazinski of Oklahoma City. Mr. Grazinski's story began when he purchased a new 32-foot Winnebago motor home. On his trip home, after entering the freeway, the Winnebago crashed and overturned.

So Grazinski sued the Winnebago Company and was awarded $1,750,000, plus a brand new recreational vehicle. This was despite the fact that, while driving home, he had set the cruise control at 70 mph and left the driver's seat to make himself a cup of coffee in the back of the Winnebago.

To be fair, Mr. Grazinski was actually suing Winnebago for not making it clear in the owner's manual that he shouldn't do that kind of thing—that is, make coffee in the back of the vehicle while leaving the driver's seat unattended. We're sure, of course, that he had read the owner's manual from cover to cover before getting into the vehicle and starting it up. (Everyone does this, right? I know I do.) Winnebago has now addressed this documentation failure by adding a sentence or two in the manual, clearly spelling out how the cruise control functions.

However, as far as I know, the Winnebago folks have not learned their lesson. They continue to leave themselves open to future litigation by anyone who happens to drive their Winnebago off the edge of a cliff, expecting it to fly, or who drives their vehicle into the sea, expecting it to turn into a submarine and sprout a periscope. I don't see either of those eventualities covered in the handbook anywhere. And believe me, I've looked.

Does this story about Mr. Grazinski sound familiar? That's possibly because it is just that—a story. Mr. Grazinski and his motor home never existed; they are, in fact, the stars of an urban legend, outed by Jan Harold Brunvand and reported by Barbara and David P. Mikkelson, the conscientious folks at Snopes.com. The snollygoster in this case is the person who invented this story and set it loose on the Internet.

All the same, you were surely a little outraged when you read the story, weren't you? Well, hold on to your hat, because this next case is the real deal.

Roy L. Pearson Jr. is an Administrative Law Judge in the Washington, D.C. area. In 2005, he sued a mom-and-pop dry cleaners run by a Korean family, the Chungs, for $65,462,500 because they lost a pair of his pants. Judge Pearson calculated the amount on the basis of every possible legal dimension of cost and damages you can imagine, and some you'd need to be a professional grimgribber to even dream up. But let's not be too harsh. Poor Judge Pearson was so distressed by the loss of his pants that, when he took the stand to testify in court, he broke down in tears.

Despite this show of emotion, the case was dismissed and damages were awarded to the dry cleaner. Having lost in the D.C. Superior Court, Judge Pearson took his case to the Court of Appeals where...he lost again! He then requested that the appeals court re-hear the case, which they refused to do.

His only possible recourse for justice now, should he choose to pursue the case, is the U.S. Supreme Court, or, failing that, The International Court of Justice in The Hague. Go for it, Roy!

Rhadamanthine

Rhadamanthus was a wise king and, according to Greek myth, the son of Zeus and Europa. Rhadamanthus and his brothers, Minos and Sarpedon, were raised by King Asterius of Crete. Following the death of Asterius, Rhadamanthus ruled over Crete justly, bequeathing it an excellent code of laws, which the Spartans are supposed to have copied. Nevertheless, siblings will be siblings and—long story short— Minos drove Rhadamanthus out of Crete. He fled to Boeotia where he married Alcmene, a granddaughter of Perseus and mother to Heracles, another of Zeus's kids. Gods will be gods.

When he died, Rhadamanthus was appointed to be one of the judges of the dead, as was his brother, Minos (the one who had so unkindly usurped him in Greece), and his half-brother, Aeacus (another of Zeus's many illegitimate offspring).

Judging the dead is a hell of a job, if you'll excuse the pun. You get to meet all kinds of people and the work is never ending, but at least the sentencing is easy. The departed soul ends up being sent to the Fields of Asphodel (you could do worse), or to the Fields of Elysium (the one to opt for if you have a choice), or to Tartarus (don't go there, just don't go there). Should you end up in Hades then you need to appreciate that Rhadamanthus is strictly and uncompromisingly just and, perhaps, a little inflexible in his application of the law. There is no point in whining about your unhappy childhood when Rhadamanthus is on the bench.

The word *rhadamanthine* is, thus, an adjective that is usually applied to hard-nosed but strictly impartial judges. For example, I would characterize Judge Judith Bartnoff as rhadamanthine in her judgment of *Pearson v. Chung*, the action (described in the previous section) that came to be known as "The Great American Pants Suit."

It was by no means an easy case. One has to admit that the plaintiff, Pearson, was clearly trying to be conciliatory when he dropped his claim for damages from over $65 million to a mere $54 million. Additionally, there was definitely a hint of public service in his suggestion that, were he to get a substantial award, he would only retain a few million for himself and would use the rest to encourage and support others in the pursuit of similar actions.

Legally, the case was crystal clear. The dry cleaners had definitely displayed a sign declaring "Satisfaction Guaranteed," and there can be little doubt that, in respect of the requested $10.50 alteration to the pair of suit pants, Pearson certainly didn't experience satisfaction. And there can be little dispute that the $1,150 that Mr. Pearson originally claimed in recompense, when the pants never turned up as expected, was rather high, but it is entirely possible that the pants had sentimental value that justified such a figure.

It's hard to quibble with Mr. Pearson's claim of $15,000 to cover the rental of a car on weekends for a period of 10 years so that that he might be able to make use of a dry cleaner in another neighborhood. And as for the bulk of the damages claim, it derived from a very plausible interpretation of Washington consumer-protection law, which imposes fines of $1,500 per violation, per day.

Since the apparently misleading "Satisfaction Guaranteed" sign had been displayed for 1,200 days and there were three defendants, the arithmetic is merciless: 3 x 1,200 x $1,500 = $5,400,000. Indeed, employing his legal knowledge, Pearson maintained that the owners were liable for seven different violations of the consumer protection act (so let's multiply $5,400,000 up a bit) and they were also guilty of fraud (so that means criminal damages, too).

And yet, despite the force of his legal arguments, the plaintiff's suit was rejected by the rhadamanthine judge on the basis that, "a reasonable consumer would not interpret *satisfaction guaranteed* to mean that a merchant is required to satisfy a customer's unreasonable demands."

Jeofail

According to most legal authority, it is axiomatic that a man who acts as his own attorney has a fool for a client. This is probably true in respect of the judge who tried to sue the pants off the people who mislaid his pants. One might expect that a judge representing himself would be sufficiently skilled in the law to provide an exception to the rule, rather than to prove the rule. However, it wasn't so. Judge Pearson committed a clear jeofail.

The whole case was predicated on the fact that the dry cleaner had irretrievably lost Pearson's pants. However, the Chungs maintained that a few days after they mislaid Judge Pearson's pants, they did indeed find them again and attempted to return them to Pearson. Pearson maintained, however, that the Chungs were trying to pull the wool over his eyes—a pair of wool pants, perhaps—with a pair that was not his. Although during the trial Pearson described in great detail "his history of community service, his weight gain as a middle-aged man, his financial woes, and his painful divorce"—all of which were possibly germane to the case—in the opinion of Judge Judith Bartnoff, he failed to prove indisputably that the pants were lost.

This was a costly legal error, which is exactly the definition of the word *jeofail*.

Dysnomy

Dysnomy is the creation of flawed legislation. The Eighteenth Amendment to the U.S. Constitution provides an excellent example of this. It is hard to argue the virtues of alcohol. It is the direct or indirect cause of hundreds of thousands of deaths in the U.S. every year. It leads to the perpetration of many minor offenses, from unacceptable public behavior to driving while intoxicated, and the social cost is enormous. Logically, banning the offending substance seems like such a good idea that it's amazing no one thought of it earlier. However, the consequences of outright prohibition of alcohol in 1920 in the U.S. were swift and disastrous, leading to a crime epidemic. The Eighteenth Amendment was repealed 14 years later, to everyone's relief.

This is not to say that the banning of alcohol is inevitably dysnomic. Alcohol is banned in quite a few countries in the Middle East, notably in Saudi Arabia, where it's prohibition leads only to minor problems. The trouble in the U.S. was that an idealistic religious minority managed, for a time, to impose laws that proved unacceptable to the stubborn drinking majority. Prohibition was dysnomic because it was impractical at that time in that place.

Utlegation

If you're familiar with Samuel Butler's poem, "Hudibras," then you will surely know the word *utlegation*. It appears in the following passage:

> "Unless, to punish them the worse,
> You put them in the secular powers
> And pass their souls, as some demise
> The same estate in mortgage twice;
> When to a legal utlegation
> You turn your excommunication
> And, for a groat unpaid that's due,
> Distrain on soul and body too."

Butler is, of course, highlighting the dichotomy between religious crime and punishment and secular crime and punishment. *Utlegation* means *outlawing*, and in his humble opinion, if you excommunicate someone, then making him an outlaw at the same time is hardly fair. It only adds insult to injury.

If Butler had not used this word, then the odds are that it would have turned up its toes and died. Aside from mentions in truly comprehensive dictionaries, that poem and this page of writing may be the only two published instances of the word in 400 years (according to Googleus, the Greek god of search).

This is a truly hybrid word because the prefix *ut* is Friesian or Germanic, but the *legation* part is unashamedly Latin. *Exlegation* would make more sense, but it doesn't exist.

Abscotchalater

If you've been utlegated you may possibly become an abscotchalater, like Magwitch in Charles Dickens' *Great Expectations*. Magwitch is the convict that Pip, the central character of the book, encounters in a churchyard. Magwitch is an abscotchalater because he's on the run from the law and Pip helps him by getting him some bread and a file to file off his shackles.

If you've not read the book or seen the movie or the TV series, then let me spoil it for you. Later in life, Pip receives a tidy sum of money from an anonymous benefactor who turns out to be Magwitch. Magwitch returns to England from Australia (it was a penal colony back in those days, and Magwitch had been transported there), but the police are after him, so he's still an abscotchalater. He has decided to spend the rest of his days with Pip, so Pip decides that he'll have to flee the country with Magwitch. To complicate matters, Magwitch is having a deadly feud with another utlegated character named Compeyson, who turns out to be the very man who swindled, jilted, and embittered Miss Haversham. Compeyson tips off the police about Magwitch, but Magwitch ends up in a brawl with him and Compeyson is killed. Magwitch gets captured, but dies before he can be hanged or sent back to Australia (whichever is worse).

Outfangtheft

As I'm sure you're aware, outfangtheft is the opposite of infangtheft. Infangtheft was the right of a Norman lord to rain down justice on any resident of his borough found guilty of theft or other such misdemeanors. Punishment was generally severe in those days, so there was the obvious temptation for wanted men to abscotchalate and move to another borough. However, by doing so they still could not escape the jurisdiction of the Norman lord due to outfangtheft, the right of the Norman lord to pursue the miscreant outside his own jurisdiction and bring him back within his jurisdiction to be punished.

It is interesting that while outfangtheft applied for centuries in Britain and elsewhere in Europe, the fundamental principle of outfangtheft was never properly established in America (between states) until the 20th century. It was then that the flight of bank robbers over state lines sparked the formation of the FBI—and the subsequent rise of the gangster movie. The only reasonable explanation for this is that the United States suffered from a severe shortage of the Norman lords needed to enforce outfangtheft.

Peccavi

Let's revisit Perry Mason and the various criminals he encountered, shall we? The most dramatic moments in those early dramas would always occur when Perry Mason had trapped some poor, miserable tortfeaser into admitting his guilt. In some of the episodes, the treacherous tortfeaser was completely submersed in denial and was carried out of the courtroom screaming his innocence. Other times, the tortfeaser would defiantly insist that the murderee earned and deserved his demise. And sometimes we were treated to a bland, almost grateful admission of guilt, the weight of the crime proving too heavy for the tortfeaser to bear. The last of these Masonic denouements is referred to as a *peccavi,* an admission of guilt.

Sir Charles Napier made the meaning of this direct-from-the-Latin word utterly clear when, in 1843, he led a small army of 2,800 British and native soldiers into Sind, a large region which is now a Southern province of Pakistan. There he won a bloody battle against a force of 22,000 Sindhis. Following the battle, he sent back a one-word dispatch to London, which read *"Peccavi"* (translated: *I have sinned*).

Some historians believe that Napier meant it both ways—*sinned* and *Sind*—since he was known to be opposed to the rampant establishment of colonies, and he's believed to have been unhappy at being ordered to do a bit of land grabbing. Either way, it was an impressive pun.

XXIII

THE LAST WORD:
PHONUS BOLONUS

"Go on, get out. Last words are for fools who haven't said enough." ~ The last recorded words of
Karl Marx (1818-1883)

Phonus bolonus is not a hobson-jobson, which is some-thing that I'm sure you'd realize immediately if you knew what a hobson-jobson was. A hobson-jobson is the alteration of a word or phrase taken from another lan-guage so that it sounds like a word of your own language. English speakers have a habit of creating hobson-jobsons. For instance, we took the perfectly good French word *ar-tichaut* and made it *artichoke*. We took the French *vin blanc* and turned it into *plonk*.

The term *hobson-jobson* comes from the excellent work, *Hobson-Jobson: A Glossary of Colloquial Anglo-Indian Words and Phrases, and of Kindred Terms, Etymological, Historical, Geographical, and Discursive*, which is pretty much what it says it is. One would think, then, that two distinguished etymologists, a Mr. Hobson and a Mr. Jobson, put this esteemed repository of knowledge together. The truth is that it was indeed put together by two distinguished ety-mologists, but their names were Henry Yule and Arthur C. Burnell.

So why *Hobson-Jobson*?

To understand this, you need to be a little familiar with the Shiite sect of Islam, which deeply reveres the Imam Hussein, the martyred grandson of the Prophet Muhammad. In the special ceremony of the Mourning of Muharram (Muharram is a month in the Islamic calendar), Shia Muslims take part in a procession, mourning the death of Imam Hussein, where they beat their chests and cry out "Ya Hasan! Ya Hosain!"

When British soldiers first watched these processions, they concluded that the Shiites were actually shouting out "Hobson! Jobson!" In time, the British in India and the Middle East referred to all unfamiliar religious festivals as Hobson-Jobsons. So *hobson-jobson*, which is itself a hobson-jobson, became the term for the absorption and corruption of foreign words.

Having said that, I confess it's a bit of a cheat to make *phonus bolonus* the last word in this book. Apart from anything else, *phonus bolonus* is two words, not one. And despite it's pretensions to the contrary, it is not Latin at all. *Phonus bolonus* is not even a hobson-jobson. If it were a Latin hobsonus-jobsonus, it would have to be *bolonus phonus*, since the Romans liked their adjectives slotted after the nouns, rather than before. If it's not Latin and it's not a hobson-jobson, then what is it?

Phonus bolonus is the American-English, faux Latinization of *phony baloney*, which is probably why you occasionally see the second part spelt *balonus*.

Phony baloney itself has a two-prong derivation. *Phony* (alternatively *phoney*) most likely came from the word *fawney*, which referred to gilded brass rings that swindlers tried to pass off as gold. This means that someone switched the natural *f* in *fawney* for the less natural *ph* in *phony*—all of which sounds like a phony explanation to me, but I can't find any other.

Baloney is usually thought of as coming from bologna sausage (from the Italian town Bologna), which is a sausage made "from this and that, and anything else that was on the table." If so, then baloney is a hobson-jobson.

However, *baloney* may also derive from the Irish word *blarney*, referring, of course, to the ancient Blarney Stone, which sits in a castle near Cork, Ireland. The Blarney Stone is supposed to bestow the gift of the gab on anyone who kisses it.

New York Governor, Alfred E. Smith, popularized the term *phony baloney* in the 1930s and, because New York has large populations of Irish and Italians, both explanations for the derivation of *baloney* are credible.

There is no record of who first added the Latin endings to *phony baloney*, but the resulting two words—*phonus bolonus*—were used by R. Crumb in comic strips published in the 1960s, and they made up the name of a Roman Centurion in the comic book series, *Asterix the Gaul*, by René Goscinny and Albert Uderzo. *Phonus bolonus*, as I'm sure you'll be relieved to know, means exactly the same as *phony baloney*.

And all of this is a kind of ingannation, since I never had any intention of making *phonus bolonus* the last word in the book.

The last word in the book is *ingannation*.

PRONUNCIATION GUIDE

CONSONANTS

[b] bobbin
[d] duck
[f] final, before
[g] gobble, bag
[h] home
[j] jacket, budge, agile
[k] cat, pack, poke
[l] loud, bellow, mile, mill
[m] morning, bummer, lime
[n] not, pine, tinny
[ng] bang, drink, strong
[p] pup, grapple
[r] rig, tarry, bar, before
[s] sin, cite, lasso, pace
[sh] shush, nation, lush
[t] too, letter, fat
[ch] change, feature, witch
[th] thought, something, worth
[*th*] there, smooth, bathe
[v] vivid
[w] wish, awake
[hw] while, everywhere
[y] yoyo, pinion
[z] zany, queasy, fuzz
[zh] leisure, vision, beige

VOWELS

[a] act, ban, sat
[ey] able, aim, late, pay, weigh
[ah] art, father, rah
[air] air, bare, tear
[aw] all, walk, cost, paw
[e] every, ahead, set
[ee] eel, easy, bee, seed
[eer] eerie, ear, zero, leer
[er] after, onward, girder
[i] itsy, wig, finicky
[ahy] I, eye, ice, wide, decry
[o] otter, shot, waffle
[oh] own, bode, goad, shallow
[oo] oodles, food, soup, sue
[*oo*] wood, foot, put
[oi] oink, coil, boy
[ou] outer, cloud, now
[uh] utter, smother, but
[*uh*] abuse, abysmal, emblem
[ur] earn, urn, gird, whirring
[œ] *feu* (French)

ABBREVIATIONS

n., noun
v., verb
adj., adjective
adv., adverb

STRESS SYLLABLES

All CAPS indicates the primary stressed syllable.

*NOTE: This pronunciation guide is borrowed from Dictionary.com and is the best of the spelt (no-symbols) pronunciation systems I've found.

173

DICTIONARY

Abacinate (*uh*-BAS-i-neyt) *v.*, to blind a person by putting a hot copper basin near the eyes (VII)

Abscotchalater (ab-SKOTCH-*uh*-leyt-ur) *n.*, a person running from the law; a person hiding from the police (XXII)

Adelphepothia (*uh*-del-f*uh*-POH-thee-*uh*) *n.*, an incestuous desire for one's sister (XIX)

Adelphirexia (*uh*-del-f*uh*-REK-see-*uh*) *n.*, an incestuous desire for one's nephew (XIX)

Adelphithymia (*uh*-del-f*uh*-THAHY-mee-*uh*) *n.*, an incestuous desire for one's niece (XIX)

Admiral (AD-mer-*uh*l) *n.*, the commander in chief of a fleet; from Arabic *amir-ar-rahl*: chief of transport (XV)

Advermation (ad-ver-MEY-shun) *n.*, information delivered as advertising on the Internet (XII)

Advertorial (ad-ver-TOHR-ee-*uh*l) *n.*, content delivered as advertising on the Internet (XII)

Aeolist (EE-*uh*-list) *n.*, a pompous bore who pretends to be inspired (XXI)

Aequeosalinocalcinosetaceoaluminosocupreovitriolic (won't even try) *n.*, a description of the spa waters, specifically at Bath, England, involving its mineralogical composition (V)

Aichmorhabdobathysiderodromophobia (eych-m*uh*-blah-blah-blah-foh-bee-*uh*) *n.*, the fear of being beaten with a pointed stick in a subway (V)

Aichmorhabdophobia (eych-m*uh*-rab-doh-foh-bee-*uh*) *n.*, the fear of being beaten with a pointed stick (V)

Aischrolatry (eys-KRAWL-*uh*-tree) *n.*, the worship of smut (XIX)

Algorithm (AL-g*uh*-rith-*uh*m) *n.*, an explicit method for solving a problem or doing something useful; eponym: Abu Abdullah Muhammad bin Musa al-Khwarizmi, 8th century Persian mathematician (VIII)

Ambulomancy (AM-byoo-l*uh*-man-see) *n.*, divination that involves watching someone walk from one place to another and gaining insight from observing the choices he or she makes en route (XIV)

Amphigony (am-FIG-*uh*-nee) *n.*, fornication (XIX)

Amphigory (AM-fi-gawr-ee) *n.*, a poem that seems profound, but is really complete nonsense (XVI)

Anemocracy (ah-n*uh*-MOK-r*uh*-see) government by whim (III)

Ankyloproctia (ang-k*uh*-loh-PROK-tee-*uh*) *n.*, stricture of the anus (XXI)

Anopisthography (ah-n*uh*-pis-THOG-r*uh*-fee) *n.*, the practice of writing on just one side of the paper (II)

Anthropomancy (an-thr*uh*-p*uh*-MAN-cee) *n.*, divination using human entrails (XIII)

Antidisestablishmentarianism (let's all chant it together…) *n.*, opposition to the separation of the state from the Church (V)

Apantomancy (ah-PANT-*uh*-man-see) *n.*, metagnomy using any object at hand (XIV)

Armomancy (ARM-*uh*-man-see) *n.*, metagnomy using a shoulder blade (normally of an animal), which has been charred from being burned in a fire; see also *omoplatoscopy* and *scapulimancy* (XIV)

Ascian (AS-ee-*uh*n) *n.*, a person or thing that has no shadow; one who inhabits the torrid zone (VII)

Astraphobia (as-tr*uh*-FOH-bee-*uh*) *n.*, fear of lightening (III)

B

Bale (beyl) *n.*, a group of turtles (X)

Balatron (BAL-*uh*-tron) *n.*, idiot (XXI)

Bathysiderodromophobia (bath-is-*uh*-der-oh-droh-m*uh*-FOH-bee-*uh* — Are you happy now?) *n.*, the fear of subways (V)

Beerocracy (bi-ROK-r*uh*-see) *n.*, government by brewers (III)

Berceuse (*Fr.* baiR-SŒZ, -s*oo*z) *n.*, a lullaby (XVII)

Betelgeuse (BEET-l-jooz) *n.*, the top left star in the constellation Orion; from Arabic *yad al jauza*: hand of the *jauza*, *jauza* being the Arabic name for the constellation Orion. (XV)

Bibliomancy (BIB-lee-oh-man-see) *n.*, another word for stichomancy, which is divination by randomly selecting a passage from a book (XIV)

Bigot (BIG-*uh*t) *n.*, a person with pronounced prejudices; eponym: Nathaniel Bigot (1575-1660), an intolerant English Puritan teacher (VIII)

Blatherskite (BLA*TH*-er-skahyt) *n.*, a garrulous talker of nonsense (XVII)

Blessing (BLES-ing) *n.*, a group of unicorns (X)

Bloomers (BLOO-merz) *n.*, women's underpants; eponym: Amelia Jenkins Bloomer (1818-94), American feminist, who never invented but did advocate the wearing of bloomers (VIII)

Bluetooth (BLOO-tooth) *n.*, the wireless protocol; eponym: Harald Blatand (c. 910-987), Viking king, whose name translates into English as *bluetooth* (VIII)

Borborygmite (bor-b*uh*-RIG-mahyt) *n.*, a person who is practiced in the use of coprophemia (XIX)

Bozon (BOH-zon) *n.*, the smallest possible quantity of stupidity that can exist independently of a body of stupidity (XII)

Brimborion (brim-BOR-ee-on) *n.*, a useless or nonsensical thing (XVII)

Brontomancy (BRON-toh-man-see) *n.*, metagnomy using thunder (XIV)

C

Cacafuego (kah-kah-FWEY-goh) *n.*, an outrageous bore (XXI)

Caitif (KEY-tif) *n.*, a despicably mean and cowardly person (XXI)

Cambronne (kam-BRON) *n.*, *Fr. merde* (XX)

Cancelmoose (KAN-s*uh*l-moos) *n.*, someone who wages war against spam (XII)

Canine (KEY-nahyn) *n.*, mammal of the genus *Canis;* derivation: Latin *canis* (IX)

Carneous (KAR-nee-*us*) *adj.*, flesh-colored (I)

Catamite (KAT-*uh*-mahyt) *n.*, a young boy kept by a pederast (XIX)

Centimorgan (SEN-t*uh*-mor-g*uh*n) *n.*, a unit of recombinant frequency for measuring genetic linkage (XI)

Ceraunomancy (s*uh*-RAW-noh-man-see) *n.*, metagnomy using lightning (XIV)

Chargoggagoggmanchauggagoggchaubunagungam-augg (as if...) *n.*, a lake in Webster, Maine, and the longest U.S. place name. In the American Indian Nipmuk language, it means: "You fish on the left side; I'll fish on the right side; no one fishes in the middle." (V)

Check (chek) *n.*, a restraint; a move in chess that directly attacks an opponent's king, but does not constitute a checkmate; the position or condition of a king so attacked. From Arabic *shah* (via Persian and Sanskrit): king; a piece in the game of chess (XV)

Chiliad (CHIL-ee-ad) *n.*, a unit containing one thousand parts or items (not a chili cook-off) (XI)

Cholangiocholecystocholedochectomy (dream on...) *n.*, a medical procedure that involves cutting out the hepatic duct, the common bile duct, and the gall bladder (V)

Circumbilivagination (ser-kum-bil-*uh*-vaj-i-NEY-sh*uh*n) *n.*, traveling or moving in a circle; walking around (V)

Cladogenesis (clad-*uh*-GEN-*uh*-sis) *n.*, evolution predicated on the existence of a common ancestor (III)

Clapperdudgeon (KLAP-er-duhj-*uh*n) *n.*, a beggar whose parents were beggars (XXI)

Cloff (kl*uh*f) *n.*, natural wastage (also spelt *clough*) (XI)

Coccydynia (kok-si-DAHY-nee-*uh*) *n.*, a pain in the coccyx (XXI)

Coffee (KAW-fee) *n.*, a caffeinated beverage made from coffee beans; from Arabic *qahwah*: coffee. Probably derives from *Kaffa*, the region of Ethiopia that is the original home of the plant (XV)

Cohyponyms (koh-HAHY-p*uh*-nim) *n.*, sibling hyponyms (XVIII)

Colubriform (k*uh*-LOO-bri-form) *adj.*, shaped like a snake (XIII)

Comma (KOM-*uh*) *n.*, a punctuation mark; eponym: Domenico de Comma (VIII)

Coprolalia (kop-roh-LEY-lee-*uh*) *n.*, the uncontrollable or obsessive use of obscene or scatological language (XIX)

Coprophemia (kop-roh-FEE-mee-*uh*) *n.*, obscene language (XIX)

Coscinomancy (k*uh*-SIN-*uh*-man-see) *n.*, metagnomy using a sieve and shears

Cromulent (KROM-yoo-l*uh*nt) *adj.*, cromulent (XVII)

Crowdsourcing (KROUD-sohrs-ing) *n.*, the situation where a task normally assigned to a member of staff or a contractor is outsourced to a poorly defined bunch of people (XII)

Cruciverbalism (kroo-s*uh*-VUR-b*uh*-liz-*uh*m) *n.*, the creation of crossword puzzles and the solving of them (XVIII)

Cubit (KYOO-bit) *n.*, 20.6 inches (Egyptian cubit) (XI)

Culacino (coo-l*uh*-SEE-noh, or -CHEE-noh) *n.*, the mark left on the table by a moist glass (VI)

Cyberagent (SAHY-ber-ey-j*uh*nt) *n.*, a person willing to work on a homeshore basis (XII)

Cyberchondria (sahy-ber-KON-dree-ak) *n.*, hypochondria caused by surfing to medical web sites that give descriptions of the symptoms of illnesses (XII)

D

Dah (dah) *n.*, a short, heavy Burmese knife (IV)

Darcy (DAHR-see) *n.*, a geological unit of measure of the permeability of rock (XI)

Dastard (DAS-terd) *n.*, a mean, cowardly, and cunning person (XXI)

Decruitment (di-KROOT-m*uh*nt) *n.*, what happens to an employee if his presenteeist efforts fail to impress; the opposite of *recruitment* (XII)

Deipnosophy (deyp-NAH-s*uh*-fee) *n.*, educated banter; specifically, learned dinner conversation (III)

Denary (DEN-*uh*-ree) *adj.*, consisting of ten parts (VI)

Diesel (DEE-zuhl) *n.*, a type of engine, a fossil fuel; eponym: Rudolf Diesel (1858-1913), German mechanical engineer who designed and built the first diesel engine (VIII)

Dog (dawg) *n.*, mammal of the genus *Canis;* derivation: *unknown* (IX)

Doggerel (DAW-ger-*uh*l) *n.*, crude verse with irregular rhythm or just plain bad poetry, often humorous; eponym: Matthew Doggerel (1330-1405), English poet, whose unappreciated poems were published by Chaucer (VIII)

Dol (dol) *n.*, the basic unit of experienced pain (XI)

Drachm (DRAHK-*uh*m) *n.*, an archaic apothecary unit of measure, equal to 3 scruples (XI)

Drudge (druhj) *n.*, a group of skeletons (X)

Dummkopf (DUM-kof) *Ger. n.*, idiot (XXI)

Dunce (duhns) *n.*, someone incapable of scholarship; eponym: John Duns Scotus (VIII)

181

Dysnomy (DIZ-n*uh*-mee) *n.*, the creation of flawed legislation (XXII)

Dysphemism (DIS-f*uh*-miz-*uh*m) *n.*, the deliberate use of a more, rather than a less, vulgar term; i.e., the opposite of a euphemism (XX)

E

Eccedentesiast (ek-s*uh*-den-TEE-zee-ast) *n.*, one faking a smile (VI)

Elixir (i-LIK-ser) *n.*, a solution of alcohol, water and syrup, often medicinal; from Arabic *al-iksir*: liquid; in alchemy, a liquid believed to confer immortality (XV)

Elozable (i-LOZ-*uh*-b*uh*l) *adj.*, amenable to flattery (Dedication)

English beer pint (beer pahynt) *n.*, 568ml (XI)

Entredentolignumologist (go for it) *n.*, a person who collects toothpick boxes (V)

Epeolatrist (eh-pee-AH-l*uh*-trist) *n.*, one who worships words (III)

Eponym (EP-*uh*-nim) *n.*, the name of a real or legendary person or thing that has been applied to an object, institution, place, era, activity, etc. (VIII)

Ergophobia (er-goh-FOH-bee-*uh*) *n.*, the fear of hard work (XVI)

Etymon (ET-*uh*-mon) *n.*, a root word from which other words derive (XX)

Excerebrose (ek-SER-*uh*-brohz) *adj.*, brainless (XXI)

Execration (ek-si-KREY-sh*uh*n) *n.*, the act of cursing, the curse itself, as well as the thing that is cursed or loathed (XX)

Exordium (eg-ZORD-yum) *n.*, introduction to a piece of writing (I)

F

Fawney (FAW-nee) *n.*, gilded brass ring that swindlers used to try to pass off as gold (XXIII)

Fescennine (FEH-s*uh*-nahyn) *adj.*, smutty, obscene, lewd, licentious and scurrilous (XIX)

Fimblefamble (FIM-b*uh*l-fam-b*uh*l) *n.*, lying excuse (I)

Floccinaucinihilipilification (you're on your own) *n.*, the categorizing of something as worthless trivia (V)

Fortuitism (for-TOO-i-*tiz*-um) *n.*, evolution by nothing more than chance variation (III)

Friendorphobia (fren-der-FOH-bee-*uh*) *n.*, the fear of forgetting a password (XII)

Fronglemenser (FRAWNG-g*uh*l-men-ser) *n.*, person who tries to engage you in conversation when you're much more interested in reading a book (I)

Furr-ahin (fur-*uh*-HIN) and **Fittie-lan** (fi-tee-LAN) *n.*, the hindmost horse on the right pulling a plough and the near horse of the hindmost pair pulling a plough, respectively (VII)

Fustilarian (foo-sti-LAIR-ee-*uh*n) *n.*, a scoudrel (XXI)

G

Galimatias (gal-i-MAH-tee-*uh*s) *n.*, something meaning-less, rather than absolutely nonsensical (XVII)

Gamogenesis (gam-*uh*-JEN-*uh*-sis) *n.*, fornication (XIX)

Gar (gahr) *n.*, a mild oath or curse (IV)

Garbist (GAR-bist) *n.*, someone who is adept at engaging in polite behavior (VI)

Garble (GAHR-b*uh*l) *v.*, to mix up or scramble; from Arabic *gharbala*: to sift (XV)

Geloscopy (jel-OS-k*uh*-pee) *n.*, metagnomy based on interpreting someone's laughter (XIV)

Gerrymander (JER-i-*man*-der) *v.*, to manipulate the boundaries and, thereby, the voting population of a voting district, in order fix or influence elections; eponym: *gerry* (Elbridge Gerry) and *salamander* (VIII)

Ginnel (GIH-n*uh*l) *n.*, alleyway (IV)

Googleganger (GOOG-*uh*l-gang-er) *n.*, someone who has the same name as you (XII)

GoogleWhacking (GOOG-*uh*l-wak-ing) *n.*, a game in which players try to find a word combination that, when entered into Google, renders only one search result (XII)

Googlomancy (GOOG-loh-man-see) *n.*, divination by typing random words into Google and interpreting the meaning of the first page link that comes up (XIV)

Gossypiboma (gah-sip-i-BOH-m*uh*) *n.*, a surgical sponge accidentally left inside a patient's body (II)

Gowk (gawk) *n.*, idiot (XXI)

Grammatolatrist (gram-*uh*-TOL-*uh*-trist) *n.*, a person who worships words (XVIII)

Grawlix (GRAW-liks) *n.*, typographical symbols used in dialogue in comics to indicate swear words (XX)

Grimgribber (GRIM-grib-ur) *n.*, a lawyer (XXII)

Grinagog (GRIN-*uh*-*gahg*) *n.*, a person who is perpetually grinning (VI)

Grizzledemundy (*griz*-l-d*uh*-MUN-dee) *n.*, a person who is perpetually grinning (VI)

Gynotikolobomassophile (gahy-no-whatever) *n.*, someone who likes to nibble on a woman's earlobe (V)

Gyromancy (JAHY-roh-man-see) *n.*, divination in which a person whose fortune is being told is put inside a circle with the alphabet's letters placed around the perimeter. The person spins around until dizzy and falls, and the letter he falls on or nearest to is noted. He continues this way—spinning and falling—until a message is spelt out. (XIV)

H

Hadeharia (heyd-*uh*-HAR-ee-*uh*) *n.*, the constant use of the word *hell* (XX)

Halidom (HAL-i-d*uh*m) *n.*, a holy or sacred object (XIII)

Harlotocracy (har-l*uh*-TOK-r*uh*-see) *n.*, government by prostitutes (III)

Haruspex (HAR-*uh*-speks) *n.*, a fortuneteller who combines the observation of lightning with the examination of entrails in her soothsaying (XIV)

Hazard (HAZ-erd) *n.*, chance, a gamble; derivation: Arabic *al zar*, dice; English, *Hazard*, a gambling game played with dice (IX)

Hellomaniac (hel-*uh*-MEY-nee-ak) *n.*, a person obsessed with foreign or unusual words (XVIII)

Helminth (HEL-minth) *n.*, an intestinal worm (XXI)

Hippopotomonstrosesquippediliophobia (haven't a clue) *n.*, fear of long words (V)

Hircismus (hur-SIS-muhs) *n.*, human armpit odor; also, the smell of a goat (XXI)

Hispid (HIS-pid) *adj.*, stubbly or unshaven (XIII)

Hobson-jobson (HOB-s*uh*n JOB-s*uh*n) *n.*, the corruption and alteration of a foreign word or phrase so that it sounds like a word of one's own language; absorption of the word or phrase into one's language (XXIII)

Homeshoring (HOHM-shor-ing) *n.*, the practice of hiring contractors who work from home, thus cutting the costs of a full-time, in-house employee (XII)

Honeyfuggle (HUN-ee-fuh-guhl) *v.*, to deceive by flattery and sweet-talk; to swindle or cheat (Dedication)

Honorificabilitudinitatibus (uhhh....) *n.*, the state of being able to achieve honors (V)

Hooligan (HOO-li-g*uh*n) *n.*, thief, ruffian; eponym: Patrick Hooligan, 19th century London-based Irish criminal, thief and ruffian (VIII)

Humgruffin (HUM-gruf-in) *n.*, a terrible person (XIII)

Hylozoist (hahy-l*uh*-ZOH-ist) *n.*, one who suspects that all matter is endowed with life (III)

Hypernym (HAHY-per-nim) *n.*, a word for a grouping that contains smaller groups; e.g., animals include mammals, mammals include cats. *Mammals* is a hypernym of *cats*, etc. See also, *hyponym* (XVIII)

Hyponym (HAHY-p*uh*-nim) *n.*, a word for a particular grouping that's part of a more general grouping; e.g., cats are mammals, mammals are animals. *Cats* is a hyponym of *mammals*. See also, *hypernym* (XVIII)

Hypothecary (hahy-PAH-th*uh*-kair-ee) *n.*, a mortgagee (II)

Hypozeuxis (hahy-p*uh*-ZOOK-sis) *n.*, a literary or rhetorical technique in which a set of parallel clauses (or sentences) is used to create a specific effect (XVIII)

I

Idiolalia (i-dee-oh-LEY-lee-*uh*) *n.*, the use of a language invented by the person using it (XVII)

Immanence (IM-*uh*-n*uh*ns) *n.*, the state of being within or not going beyond a given domain; the pervading presence of God in His creation (XVI)

Immaterialism (im-*uh*-TEER-ee-*uh*-liz-*uh*m) *n.*, the theory that material substance does not exist and the universe is created by the mind and its ideas (XVI)

Infotisement (in-foh-TAHYZ-m*uh*nt) *n.*, information delivered as advertising on the Internet (XII)

Infracaninophile (in-fr*uh*-k*uh*-NAHYN-*uh*-fahyl) *n.*, someone who supports the underdog (XIII)

Ingannation (in-g*uh*-NEY-sh*uh*n) *n.*, deception (XXIII)

J

Jabberknowl (JAB-er-nawl) *n.*, idiot (XXI)

Jementous (j*uh*-MEN-tuhs) *adj.*, smelling of horse urine (XXI)

Jentacular (jen-TAK-yoo-ler) *adj.*, related to breakfast (II)

Jeofail (GEE-*uh*-feyl) *n.*, a costly legal error (XXII)

Jigget (JIH-git) *n.*, a unit consisting of 20 sheep (XI)

Joola (JOO-l*uh*) *n.*, a suspension bridge built out of ropes that crosses a chasm (XIII)

K

Kalling (KAL-ing) *n.*, metagnomy based on the variety of cabbage a blindfolded person picks up when several are arrayed in front of him (XIV)

Kef (kehf) *n.*, a dreamy state (IV)

L

Lalochezia (ley-loh-KEEZ-ee-*uh*) *n.*, the use of foul language in response to sudden stress or pain (XX)

Latrinalia (la-tr*uh*-NEYL-ee-*uh*) *n.*, words, markings or other graffiti inscribed on restroom walls (XX)

Lethologica (leh-th*uh*-LOH-*ji*-k*uh*) *n.*, the inability to find the right word for something (III)

Lexiphanicist (leks-i-FAN-*uh*-sist) *n.*, a person who shows off by using an extensive vocabulary (XVIII)

Lief (leef) *adv.*, soon, gladly (IV)

Llanfairpwllgwyngyllgogerychwyrndrobwllllantysiliogogogoch (I'm never going to visit, so why bother?) *n.*, a village in Wales and the longest place name in the UK. The name means, "St. Mary's Church in the hollow of the white hazel near to the rapid whirlpool of Llantysilio of the Red Cave." (V)

Loganamnosis (lohg-*uh*-NAM-*noh*-sis) *n.*, a condition in which one focuses so intently on trying to remember a word as to be unable to continue in conversation (VI)

Logarithmancy (law-g*uh*-RI*TH*-man-see) *n.*, divination using algorithms, specifically logarithms; in general, divination that employs sophisticated mathematics (XIV)

Logastellus (lawg-*uh*-STEL-uhs) *n.*, a person whose love of words exceeds their knowledge of words (XVIII)

Logomaniac (lawg-*uh*-MEY-nee-ak) *n.*, a person who is crazy about words (XVIII)

Longiloquence (lawng-IL-*uh*-kwens) *n.*, the practice of using far too many words to make one's point (XVI)

Lopadotemachoselachogaleokranioleipsanodrimhy-
potrimmatosilphioparaomelitokatakechymeno-
kichlepikossyphophattoperisteralektryonoptekeph-
alliokigklopeleiolagoiosiraiobaphetraganopterygon
(*yikes!*) *n.*, a ghoulash composed of all the leftovers
from the meals of the last two weeks (V)

Lubberland (LUB-er-*land*) *n.*, a mythical paradise
reserved for those who are lazier than a pillow tester
(VI)

Lynch (linch) *v.*, to hang a person without a trial; eponym: unknown, but there are many contenders (VIII)

M

Macaronics (mak-*uh*-RON-iks) *n.*, the mixing of Latin
words with other words from normal language, in
prose or poetry, to produce semi-profound nonsense
(XVII)

Macrologist (mak-ROL-*uh*-jist) *n.*, a boring conversationalist (VI)

Macromancy (MAK-roh-man-see) *n.*, metagnomy by
studying the largest object in the area (XIV)

Magazine (mag-uh-ZEEN) *n.*, contents of a storehouse,
especially a stock of ammunition; from Arabic
makhazin: storehouse (XV)

Maledictaphobia (mal-*uh*-dik-t*uh*-FOH-bee-*uh*) *n.*, the
fear of saying bad words (XVIII)

Mallemaroking (MAL-*uh*-m*uh*-roh-king) *n.*, the carousing of seamen in icebound Greenland whaling ships
(VII)

Marmalade (MAHR-m*uh*-leyd) *n.*, a clear, jellylike
preserve made from the pulp and rind of fruits, usually citrus; eponym: Joao Marmalado from Portugal

(1450-1510), who learned to boil oranges with sugar and water (VIII)

Maverick (MAV-er-rik, MAV-rik) *n.*, an unbranded range animal, typically a calf; eponym: Samuel Augustus Maverick, American pioneer rancher (VIII)

Megalithic yard (meg-*uh*-LITH-ik yard) *n.*, 2.72 feet (XI)

Meronym (MAIR-*uh*-nim) *n.*, a word that refers to something that's part of something else. For example, *claw* is a meronym in respect of *lion*. See also, *hyponym* and *hypernym* (XVIII)

Metagnomy (meh-TAG-n*uh*m-ee) *n.*, another word for divination (XIV)

Metonymy (meh-TON-*uh*-mee) *n.*, a figure of speech in which one noun or phrase steps in for another; e.g., *White House* is a metonym of *President*. This usage is an example of metonymy. (XVIII)

Mew (myoo) *v.*, to moult; to make a sound like a cat (IV)

Mho (MOH) *n.*, a unit of electrical conductance equivalent to the reciprocal of one ohm (XVIII)

Micromancy (MAHYK-roh-man-see) *n.*, metagnomy by studying the smallest object in the area (XIV)

Militaster (MIL-*uh*-teys-ter) *n.*, a soldier with no skills or ability (XIII)

Milquetoast (MILK-tohst) *n.*, a meek, unassertive person (typically applied to a man) (XXI)

Misocainea (mi-soh-KEY-nee-*uh*) *n.*, the obsessive hatred of anything new or strange (XVI)

Mobisode (MOH-*uh*-sohd) *n.*, an episode of a broadcast television program that has been converted for viewing on a mobile device (XII)

Monsoon (mon-SOON) *n.*, the seasonal wind of the Indian Ocean and southern Asia; derivation: a combination of the Portuguese *monção*, the rainy season in East Asia, and the Arabic *mawsim*, the appropriate season for a voyage or pilgrimage (XV)

Mooreeffoc (MAWR-ee-foc) *n.*, the strangeness of things that have become trite, when they are seen suddenly from a new angle (XVIII)

Morpheme (MAWR-feem) *n.*, the smallest meaningful unit in the grammar of a language (XVIII)

Mow (moh) *v.*, to grimace, to cut grass (IV)

Murmuration (mur-m*uh*-REY-sh*uh*n) *n.*, a group of starlings (X)

Mutchkin (MUHCH-kin) *n.*, 426ml, a quantity of beer in Scotland, which represents a quarter of a Scottish pint (XI)

Myriad (MIR-ee-*uh*d) *n.*, a very large but indeterminate number (XI)

N

Neverthriving (nev-er-THRAHYV-ing) *n.*, a group of jugglers (X)

Nicotine (NIK-*uh*-teen) *n.*, an alkaloid found in tobacco leaves; eponym: Jean Nicot, French ambassador to Portugal (1559-1561) (VIII)

Nincompoop (NIN-k*uh*m-poop) *n.*, idiot (XXI)

Ninnyhammer (NIN-ee-ham-er) *n.*, idiot (XXI)

Nosism (NOH-siz-*uh*m) *n.*, the practice of referring to oneself in the first person plural, "we" (VI)

Noxal (NOKS-ul) *adj.*, of or pertaining to damage or wrongful injury from an object, animal, or other living thing belonging to someone else (II)

O

Ohnosecond (oh-noh-SEK-*uh*nd) *n.*, the time it takes a person to realize they've just goofed by doing something stupid on a computer; e.g., forgetting to attach a document to an email or accidentally sending an email to an unintended recipient (XII)

Omoplatoscopy (om-*uh*-pl*uh*-TOS-k*uh*-pee) *n.*, metagnomy using a shoulder blade (normally of an animal), charred in a fire (I and XIV)

Onomatomania (ahn-*uh*-mah-t*uh*-MEY-nee-*uh*) *n.*, intense concentration on certain words and their supposed significance, or on the effort to recall a particular word; extreme vexation at having difficulty finding the right word (VI)

Onomatophobia (on-*uh*-mah-t*uh*-FOH-bee-*uh*) *n.*, the fear of hearing a certain word (XVIII)

Ornithoscelidaphobia (awr-n*uh*-th*uh*-sel-*uh*-d*uh*-FOH-bee-*uh*) *n.*, the fear of dinosaurs (VII)

Outfangtheft (out-FANG-theft) *n.*, the right of a (Norman) lord to pursue a miscreant outside his own jurisdiction and bring him back within his jurisdiction to be punished (XXII)

P

Paleographist (pey-lee-OG-r*uh*-fist) *n.*, an expert in the study of ancient writing (XIII)

Pancosmism (pan-KOZ-mi-z*uh*m) *n.*, the theory that the whole of existence comprises only the physical universe (XVI)

Panic (PAN-ik) *n.*, sudden fright without any visible cause; eponym: the Greek god Pan (VIII)

Paranym (PAR-*uh*-nim) *n.*, a euphemism. See also, *paronym* (XVIII)

Pareunia (p*uh*-ROO-nee-*uh*) *n.*, fornication (XIX)

Paronym (PAR-*uh*-nim) *n.*, a word allied to another word by derivation from the same root, a homonym wannabe; e. g., *deprecate* and *depreciate*. See also, *paranym* (XVIII)

Pasquinade (pas-kw*uh*-NEYD) *n.*, a parody either in verse or prose, often anonymous (XVII)

Peccavi (p*uh*-KAH-wee) *Latin n.*, an admission of guilt (XXII)

Penphobia (pen-FOH-bee-*uh*) *n.*, the morbid fear of writing or of the written word (XVIII)

Pentapopemptic (pen-t*uh*-p*uh*-PEMP-tik) *adj.*, divorced five times (VII)

Permalancer (PER-m*uh*-lan-ser) *n.*, a freelancer who hangs around forever (XII)

Philalethe (fil-*uh*-LEE-thee) *n.*, someone who forgets things, and does so with great enthusiasm; someone who loves forgetting (XVI)

Phobologophobia (foh-b*uh*-loh-g*uh*-FOH-*bee*-uh) *n.*, the fear of words about fears (VII)

Phon (fon) *n.*, a subjective measure of loudness (XI)

Phonus bolonus (FOH-n*uh*s b*uh*-LOH-n*uh*s) *n.*, phony baloney (XXIII)

Pigmentocracy (pig-men-TOK-r*uh*-see) *n.*, government by those of one skin color (II)

Pleonasm (PLEE-*uh*-naz-*uh*m) *n.*, a redundant word or phrase; redundancy in words (XV)

Pneumonoultramicroscopicsilicovolcanoconiosis (noo-mon-oh-something) *n.*, a coal-mining disease (V)

Pod (pod) *n.*, a group of whales (X)

Poliadic (pol-ee-AD-ik) *adj.*, relating to a local deity (XIII)

Poltroon (pol-TROON) *n.*, a coward; originally, a lazy and cowardly person (XXI)

Poodle-faker (POOD-l-*fey*-ker) *n.*, a young man who seeks advancement through his association with women, particularly with women who are wealthy or of higher social status (VII)

Porphyrophobia (pawr-*feer*-uh-FOH-*bee-uh*) *n.*, the fear of the color purple (VII)

Portmanteau word (port-man-TOH wurd) *n.*, a word composed by a concatenation and condensation of two words, with elements and meanings of each packed into one new word (XVIII)

Portmantologist (port-man-TOL-*uh*-jist) *n.*, a person who studies or coins portmanteau words. See *portmanteau word* (XVIII)

Presenteeism (prez-*uh*n-TEE-iz-*uh*m) *n.*, the practice of working extra hours and skipping holidays in order to try to preserve one's job (XII)

Proctalgia (prok-TAL-j*uh*) *n.*, a pain in the rectal muscle (XXI)

Prolegomenon (pro-l*uh*-GOM-i-non) *n.*, introduction to a piece of writing (I)

Pseudoantidisestablishmentarianism (soo-doh-etc-etc) *n.*, a feigned opposition to the separation of the state from the Church (V)

Pulpititude (PUHL-pi-tood) *n.*, a group of preachers (X)

Punch (puhnch) *n.*, a mixed drink, usually with alcohol; derivation: Hindi *paantsch*, five (IX)

Pygalgia (pahy-GAL-*juh*, pi-) *n.*, pain in the buttocks (XXI)

Q

Quadriliteral (kwod-r*uh*-LIT-er-*uh*l) *n.*, a four-letter word (XX)

Qualtagh (KWAWL-tahg) *n.*, the first person you run into after you leave your house (XVI)

Quarantine (KWAWR-*uh*n-teen) *n.*, restriction period invoked by authorities to protect a healthy population from those suspected of carrying disease; derivation: Italian *quaranténa*, a period of 40 days (IX)

Quickhatch (KWIK-hatch) *n.*, a wolverine (II)

Quintessential (kwin-t*uh*-SEN-sh*uh*l) *adj.*, the very essence of; derivation: Latin *quinta essentia*, fifth essence, posited by Aristotle as the fifth element (IX)

Quomodocunquize (kw*uh*-moh-doh-KUN-kwahyz) *v.*, to make money by any possible means (II)

R

Rampallian (ram-PAL-y*uh*n) *n.*, a mean wretch (XXI)

Rectalgia (rek-TAL-j*uh*) *n.*, a pain in the rectum (XXI)

Remplissage (rawm-pli-SAHZH) *n.*, padding; extraneous material, usually meaningless or nonsensical, added to literary or musical works (XVII)

Renifleur (ren-*uh*-FLUR) *n.*, someone who gets sexual pleasure from body smells (XIX)

Resistentialism (ri-zi-STEN-sh*uh*-liz-*uh*m) *n.*, the spiteful behavior of inanimate things (XIII)

Retromancy (RE-troh-man-see) *n.*, metagnomy by looking over one's shoulder (XIV)

Retronym (RE-troh-nim) *n.*, a word or words created to supersede other words that have become outdated by events, in order to bring them up to date; a word constructed from another word spelt backwards (XVIII)

Rhadamanthine (rad-*uh*-MAN-theen) *adj.*, hard-nosed but strictly impartial, usually applied to judges; derivation: *Rhadamanthus*, mythical Greek king who, because he was a wise and impartial man, was appointed by Zeus to judge the dead. (XXII)

Rhapsodomancy (rap-SOH-d*uh*-man-see) *n.*, divination by randomly selecting a passage from a book of poetry (XIV)

Rigel (RAHY-juhl) *n.*, the star marking the foot of Orion in the constellation Orion; from Arabic *rijl*: foot. (XV)

Robot (ROH-bot) *n.*, an artificial person; derivation: 1920 play, *Rossum's Universal Robots,* by Karel Capek; Czech *robota*, work, compulsory labor (IX)

Runcible (RUN-si-b*uh*l) *adj.*, the meaning of this word is unknown, except to its inventor, Edward Lear (XVII)

S

Sahara (suh-HAR-*uh*, suh-HAIR-*uh*) *n.*, a vast desert in Northern Africa; derivation: Arabic *cahara*, desert (XV)

Salary (SAL-*uh*-ree) *n.*, remuneration for work; derivation: Latin *sal*, salt (IX)

Salient (SEY-lee-*uh*nt) *adj.*, important, something that jumps out; derivation: Latin *salire,* to jump (IX)

Salmonella (sal-m*uh*-NEL-*uh*) *n.*, a hog cholera bacillus; eponym: Elmer Salmon (1850-1914), American veterinary surgeon (VIII)

Saracen (SAR-uh-suhn) *n.*, a member of any nomadic tribe in the Mid-east, a Muslim from the time of the Crusades; derivation: Arabic *sharquiyin,* east (XV)

Scapulimancy (SKAP-yoo-l*uh*-man-see) *n.*, metagnomy using a shoulder blade (normally of an animal), which has been charred from being burned in a fire; see also *omoplatoscopy* and *armomancy* (XIV)

Scatolinguistics (skat-oh-ling-GWIS-tiks) *n.*, the study of the etymology and usage of all vulgar and profane expressions (XX)

Schnook (shn*oo*k) *n.*, idiot (XXI)

Schoenobatic (skee-n*uh*-BAT-ik) *adj.*, relating to balance, specifically, to tightrope walking (XIII)

Scottish beer pint (beer pahynt) *n.*, 1,704ml, equal to 3 English beer pints (XI)

Scriptophobia (skrip-t*uh*-FOH-bee-*uh*) *n.*, the morbid fear of writing or of the written word (XVIII)

Scruple (SKROO-p*uh*l) *n.*, a British unit of weight equal to 20 grains or one-third of a drachm (XI)

Scullion (SKUHL-y*uh*n) *n.*, a low-ranking domestic servant who performs menial kitchen tasks; derivation: French *escouillon,* a swab or cloth (XXI)

Selcouth (SEL-kooth) *adj.*, strange, unfamiliar, marvelous, wondrous (XVI)

Sevidical (s*uh*-VID-i-k*uh*l) *adj.*, speaking cruel and harsh words (XVIII)

Silhouette (sil-oo-ET) *n.*, outline of an object that is cast by its shadow, typically of a person's profile; eponym: Etienne de Silhouette, French finance minister (1709-1767) (VIII)

Sin (sin) *n.*, a transgression; multiple derivations, including: Old English *synn*, Old Norse *synd*, German *Sünde* – a crime, evil doing; Latin *peccatum*, religious error; Greek *hamartia*, to miss the target; Hebrew *het*, to err, miss the mark (IX)

Sloth (slawth) *n.*, a group of bears (X)

Slubberdegullion (sluhb-er-d*uh*-GHUL-y*uh*n) *n.*, a slobbering foul individual, a worthless sloven, a pigpen, a jeeter, a tramp, an uncouth, a disgusting draggletail, and a torpid and tawdry tatterdemalion—in other words, a slob (XXI)

Slug (sluhg) *n.*, a unit of gravitational mass equal to the mass that accelerates at 1 foot per second per second when acted upon by a force of 1 pound, which means that it has an apparent weight of 32.174 pounds (XI)

Sneak (sneek) *n.*, a group of weasels (X)

Snollygoster (SNOL-ee-gos-ter) *n.*, a shrewd, unprincipled individual (XXII)

Snup (snuhp) *v.*, to buy something of value, which a less discerning person has discarded or sold cheap (IV)

Sophisticated (s*uh*-FIS-ti-key-tid) *adj.*, technically superior; derivation: Greek *sophos*, wisdom (IX)

Sortes Homerica (sor-teys hoh-MAIR-ik-*uh*) *n.*, *(Latin)* divination by randomly selecting a passage from *The Iliad* (XIV)

Sortes Virgilianae (sor-teys vir-jil-ee-EY-nahy) *n.*, *(Latin)* divination by randomly selecting a passage from *The Aeneid* (XIV)

Spurcitious (spur-SI-sh*uh*s) *adj.*, foul or obscene (XIX)

Squaliform (SKWAH-li-form) *adj.*, shark-shaped (II)

Steatopygous (stee-at-*uh*-PAHY-g*uh*s) *adj.*, having an extreme accumulation of fat on or about the buttocks (XXI)

Stichomancy (STIK-oh-man-see) *n.*, divination by randomly selecting a passage from a book (XIV)

Stork (stawrk) *n.*, a large, white bird of the crane family with long, stick-like legs; derivation: German *storch*, stick (IX)

Supercalifragilisticexpialidocious (it's better when Dick Van Dyke sings it…) *n.*, a word that is properly used only if you can't think of anything to say (V)

Superfluity (soo-per-FLOO-i-tee) *n.*, a group of nuns (X)

Suq (sook) *n.*, also *souk:* a Middle Eastern market (IV)

Sutler (SUT-ler) *n.*, a camp follower, one who hangs around the army to sell provisions to the soldiers (IV)

Syphilis (SIF-*uh*-lis) *n.*, a venereal disease; eponym: a character in the poem, "Syphilis sive Morbus Gallicus," by Girolamo Fracastro (1483-1553), both the name of a shepherd and his disease (VIII)

T

Taghairm (TAG-hairm) *n.*, metagnomy in which a person with a question about the future is wrapped in the hide of an ox and placed in the recess of a waterfall or at the bottom of a precipice to lie in wait for an answer to come to him through inspiration (XIV)

Tawdry (TAW-dree) *adj.*, tatty, cheap; derivation: English *St. Audrey*, 7th century saint (IX)

Teergrube (TEER-groo-b*uh*) *n., (German)* tar pit (XII)

Tetrapyloctomy (teh-tr*uh*-pahy-LOK-t*uh*-mee) *n.*, the splitting of hairs four ways (III)

Thygatrilagnia (thahy-g*uh*-tri-LAG-nee-*uh*) *n.*, an incestuous desire for one's daughter (XIX)

Thymogenic (thahy-moh-GEN-ik) *adj.*, generated by emotion (III)

Tmesis (t*uh*-MEE-sis) *n.*, the practice of breaking a word in two and inserting another word in the middle, usually for emphasis; e.g., the British exclamation: "abso-bloody-lutely" (XVIII)

Tod (tod) *n.*, a measure for wool equal to 28 pounds (XI)

Tortfeaser (TORT-feez-er) *n.*, a wrongdoer (XXII)

Tot (tot) *n.*, a bone or some other object one might retrieve from a pile of garbage (IV)

Tranche (trawnch) *n., (French)* slice (II)

Tribadism (TRIB-*uh*-diz-*uh*m) *n.*, lesbianism (XIX)

U

Ultracrepidate (uhl-tr*uh*-KREP-i-deyt) *v.*, criticize beyond one's sphere of knowledge (III)

Umami (oo-MAH-mee) *n.*, the taste of meat (III)

Unkindness (uhn-KAHYND-nes) *n.*, a group of ravens (X)

Utlegation (ut-l*uh*-GEY-sh*uh*n) *n.*, outlawing; conferring the status of outlaw on a convicted criminal (XXII)

V

Varietist (VAIR-ee-*uh*-tist) *n.*, one who has unorthodox sexual practices (XIX)

Verbigerate (ver-BIG-er-eyt) *v.*, to repeat nonsense or clichés (XVII)

Verbivore (VUR-b*uh*-vohr) *n.*, a person who devours words (XVIII)

Verbolatrist (vur-BOL-*uh*-trist) *n.*, a person who worships words (XVIII)

Verbophobe (VUR-b*uh*-fohb) *n.*, a person who lives in fear of words (XVIII)

Vilipend (VIL-*uh*-pend) *v.*, to disparage others (VI)

Viraginity (vir-*uh*-JIN-i-tee) *n.*, the masculine qualities of a woman (XIII)

W

Wan (wahn) *n.*, *(Mandarin Chinese)* 10,000 (XI)

Webliography (web-lee-OG-r*uh*-fee) *n.*, a compilation of web sources and resources used in the research of this book. *Webliography* is a portmanteau word, coined by this author (XVIII)

Wegotism (WEE-goh-tiz-*uh*m) *n.*, the excessive use of 'we' (first person plural) in writing, but not in speech (VI)

Wen (wehn) *n.*, a sebacious cyst; a spongy headgrowth that some goldfish have; a character from the Old English alphabet derived from a rune; a highly congested city (IV)

Wisteria (wi-STEER-ee-*uh*) *n.*, a woody vine of the genus *Wisteria,* which has fragrant, pendant clusters of purplish or white flowers; eponym: conflicting accounts credit the name to Caspar Wistar, physician (1761-1818), or Daniel Wister, noted Quaker businssman (1738-1805) (VIII)

X

Xenobombulation (zen-*uh*-bom-byoo-LEY-shun) *n.*, the act of avoiding ones duties (II)

Xenoglossy (zen-*uh*-GLAW-see) *n.*, the ability to speak a language without having learned it (VII)

Y

Yare (yehr) *adj.*, nimble, alert, prepared (IV)

Z

Zany (ZEY-nee) *adj.*, endearingly comical, buffoonish; eponym: Zanni, one of the comedic characters of the Commedia dell'arte (VIII)

Zoic (ZOH-ik) *adj.*, containing evidence of life (IV)

Zumbooruk (ZOOM-*boo*-ruk) *n.*, a cannon fired from the back of a camel (VII)

Zygopleural (zahy-g*uh*-PLOOR-*uh*l) *adj.*, having bilateral symmetry (VII)

Webliography

None of the research done in the writing of this book actually involved printed matter. The following is a list of sites that were used in one way or another as language resources and for source material. The web links can be accessed directly on WordsYouDontKnow.com by clicking on the links tab or by entering the URL *http://wordsyoudontknow.com/links/webliography/*

ENCYCLOPEDIA

The Wikipedia
Wikipedia is so comprehensive I rarely use anything else as a first research resource. (URL *http://www.wikipedia.org/*)

DICTIONARIES

One Look Dictionary Search
In my experience this is by far the most useful dictionary site on the web. It allows you to search a multitude of dictionaries at once. Also, you can put wild card entries in, such as *ace, which will give you all entries ending in -*ace*. (URL *http://onelook.com/*)

The Concise Oxford English Dictionary (OED)
This site has a search that provides access to the *Concise Oxford English Dictionary*. It also has many other useful English resources. Access to the full OED is by subscription only. (URL *http://www.askoxford.com/?view=uk*)

The Merriam Webster Dictionary
Just as the *Oxford English Dictionary* constitutes what is generally regarded as the best British dictionary, the *Merriam Webster Dictionary* constitutes what is generally re-

garded as the best American dictionary. (URL *http://www.merriam-webster.com/dictionary/*)

The Wiktionary

Although far less well known than the Wikipedia, the Wiktionary is an excellent resource. Unusually it provides English definitions of foreign language words and even Ancient language words. So if you enter the Latin word *bellum*, it will inform you that this means *war*. (URL *http://en.wiktionary.org/wiki/Wiktionary:Main_Page*)

Cambridge Dictionaries

This is a British dictionary and useful because it offers both a dictionary of phrases (that use a specific word) and a dictionary of American English. (URL *http://dictionary.cambridge.org/*)

American Heritage Dictionary of the English Language

This is a Yahoo! capability and is very comprehensive. Recommended. (URL *http://education.yahoo.com/reference/dictionary/entry/*)

Dictionary.com

This is Ask.com's dictionary capability. Also very comprehensive, with a very accessible pronunciation guide, as well as an excellent associated Thesaurus and Reference. (URL*http://dictionary1.classic.reference.com/search?*)

Webster's Unabridged Dictionary 1913

A searchable version of a truly comprehensive copyright-expired dictionary. (URL *http://www.bibliomania.com/b/OldUrlRedirect/Reference/Webster/index.html*)

RhymeZone Rhyming Dictionary

Not only good for rhymes, but also synonyms and homophones. (URL *http://www.rhymezone.com/*)

SOURCES FOR ETYMOLOGY

Some of the Dictionary sources listed in this webliography offer etymological notes along with the definitions of words. The following resources can also be useful:

Online Etymological Dictionary

I use this as my primary source of etymology. It's not especially good for obscure words, but very good for just about everything else. (URL *http://www.etymonline.com/index.php?e*)

Etymologically Speaking

This is not a comprehensive resource, but it does list a good many words with curious word origins. (URL *http://www.westegg.com/etymology/*)

English Words Derived from Latin-Greek Origins

Good for Latin and Greek etymology. (URL *http://www.wordexplorations.com/*)

QUOTATIONS

WorldofQuotes.com

A good, no-nonsense quotes site. Recommended. (URL *http://www.worldofquotes.com/*)

The Quote Garden

Very useful and nicely laid out site. (URL *http://www.quotegarden.com/*)

Bibliomania

Useful site because it has Grocott's Quotations complete and searchable. (URL *http://www.bibliomania.com/*)

Creative Wit

Good source of humorous quotes. (URL *http://creativewit.com/searchcqwit.htm*)

Bartlett's Familiar Quotations
An older version of the classic quotations resource, which is now in the public domain. (URL *http://www.bartleby.com/99/*)

UNUSUAL WORDS

I have built my own collection, but there are others out there that I've consulted. They include:

The Phrontistery
Word lists on various topics, very intelligently arranged. (URL *http://phrontistery.info/index.html*)

Grandiloquent Dictionary
Another list of unusual words, now in its third edition. (URL *http://www.islandnet.com/%7Eegbird/dict/dict.htm*)

Luciferous Logolepsy
A very large compilation of strange, rarely used words. (URL *http://www.kokogiak.com/logolepsy/*)

SKB's List o' Nifty Words
Another good list of obscure words. (URL *http://stommel.tamu.edu/%7Ebaum/skb_dict.html*)

ABOUT THE AUTHOR

Robin Bloor is not and never has been a philologist, glottologist, grammarian, lexicographer or linguist. Insofar as he has qualifications, they are in Computer Science and Mathematics. Admittedly, though, he is a published author. He has written a business book (*The Electronic B@zaar*) and co-authored several Dummies books, published by Wiley Publishing, Inc., on the subject of computer technology. He is also a public speaker, having presented to audiences on every continent except the cold one, but those presentations were done in the guise of technology expert, not English Language dilettante.

Nevertheless, an English Language dilettante is what he has become, and consequently he has written a book to prove it. The motivation for this is accidental. He is the author of the blog, HaveMacWillBlog.com, and has pursued blogging with some enthusiasm. Having taken to the keyboard in this way, he decided to write about anything and everything that came to mind—not just technology, but also his travels, poetry, weird ideas, photography and even politics.

One day in April, he started writing about strange and obscure words and it attracted a bigger audience than usual, so he continued to do it until he'd accumulated sufficient material for this book.

Since writing the book, his web site has split like an amoeba and he's now a doppleblogger, banging out words on a regular basis for his new site, WordsYouDontKnow.com. You will find further writings of the kind in this book on that site.

If you want to follow Robin Bloor on twitter, and we have no idea why you would, his id is robinbloor.

He's an Englishman currently living in Austin, Texas.

Lightning Source UK Ltd.
Milton Keynes UK
UKOW02f1809260916

283865UK00001B/10/P